Gourmet Ireland

Companion to the Public Television Series

Gourmet Ireland

Paul and Jeanne Rankin

KQED
BOOKS

San Francisco

Note for Vegetarians:

Recipes suitable for vegetarians are marked with a (V) symbol. Please note that these may include cheese and other dairy products.

First published 1994 by BBC Books. This edition published 1997 by KQED Books, by arrangement with BBC Books, a division of BBC Worldwide, Ltd.

Publisher: James Connolly
Editorial Director: Pamela Byers
Art Director: Jeffrey O'Rourke
Editor for North American edition: Sharon Silva
Editorial assistance: Liza Wachman
Cover and book design: Shelly Meadows/Homefire
Food photographs: Graham Kirk
Cover portrait: Tim Wainwright

Educational and nonprofit groups wishing to order this book at attractive quantity discounts may contact: KQED Books & Video, 555 DeHaro St., San Francisco, CA 94107.

Library of Congress Cataloguing-in-Publication Data

Rankin, Paul.
    Gourmet Ireland / Paul & Jeanne Rankin.
        p.   cm.
    Originally published: London: BBC Books. 1994
    Includes index.
    ISBN 0-912333-15-4
    1. Cookery, Irish.   I. Rankin, Jeanne.   II. Gourmet Ireland
    (Television program)   III. Title.
    TX717.5.R36   1997
    641.59416--dc21   97-192
                                CIP

Manufactured in Hong Kong
10 9 8 7 6 5 4 3 2 1

On the cover: Warm Game Tart with Roasted Winter Vegetables, Page 89; Roast Partridge with Bacon, Garlic, and Thyme, Page 85; Ring of Kerry, Ireland, © W.L. Bursenbrugge/Superstock.

Distributed to the trade by Publishers Group West

Contents

About the Authors

Paul Rankin, from County Down, Northern Ireland, and **Jeanne,** born in Minneapolis, Minnesota, and raised in Winnipeg, Canada, met while working on a boat in Greece. They were both twenty and traveling the world. To finance their journeys they worked as waiters and in restaurant kitchens, but cooking soon became their passion. On the advice of a French chef in Australia, they went to London for professional training and were taken on by Albert Roux, Paul at La Gavroche and Jeanne at Le Poulbort and Gavvers. In 1984 they married and in 1986, with their first child, they moved to Canada. A year later Paul took charge of the kitchens of the Mountview Hotel in Calistoga, California. Here, for the first time, he was able to develop his own ideas for recipes and presentation.

The Rankins returned to Ireland in 1989 with their two daughters, bought a bankrupt Belfast restaurant, and Roscoff was born. In a city where there was a shortage of outstanding restaurants, it soon made its name and has continued to break new culinary ground, while the Rankins have become well-known as two of the most creative and popular chefs working in the United Kingdom today.

Acknowledgments

We take this opportunity to thank **Brian Waddell,** producer of the *Gourmet Ireland* TV series. Without his inspiration it might never have been. We would also like to thank **Maria McCann,** the assistant producer, and all the film crew.

We owe a great deal to the wonderful **growers, producers, and suppliers,** whom we met when making the televisions series, for their knowledge and time, their devotion and energy. We truly thank all of them, too numerous to list here.

Our gratitude extends to **John and Sally McKenna,** whose research and knowledge helped so much to develop the Irish food scene.

Finally, and most important of all, **the staff at Roscoff,** our restaurant in Belfast, deserve our heartfelt thanks, for their hard work and support over the years.

Introduction

Gourmet Ireland. To many people these two words are a contradiction in terms. In their minds, food in Ireland conjures up heaps of overcooked meat piled up on a plate with underseasoned boiled root vegetables alongside—nothing "gourmet" about it. But Irish cooking and Irish food do not necessarily mean the same thing.

When we were first asked to suggest a concept for a cooking program, it was the food products of this island that got us really excited. Here was something that we felt more people had to know about. We ourselves were typical of those who wrongly stereotyped images of Irish food. In 1989 we returned to Belfast from the Napa Valley in California. Out there, a chef is swamped with choice; everything is available, nothing is a problem. As we worked feverishly at getting the doors of Roscoff open, we worried that we would not be able to obtain products that would be of a good enough quality. After all, we had just come from one of the food world's most exciting and progressive hot spots. Could a small island like Ireland ever measure up to such a developed hub?

To say that we were in for a pleasant surprise is an understatement, and we still, nearly five years later, marvel at the true state of affairs. The more we look, the more we find. There is an absolute gold mine of products, and hand in hand a wealth of people working to develop and supply them. It is these growers, producers, and suppliers that should be encouraged and supported, and we decided that, in our television series and our book, we had the opportunity to do just that.

To film the series we traveled all over Ireland, from the green glens of Antrim in the north to the rich pasturelands of County Cork in the south, from the fishing ports along the coasts to the colorful markets of inland towns up and down the country, talking and tasting, seeing and learning. We wanted to discover just what was being done on this little island in the name of food. We found that things in Ireland are on the move. The people in the industry—be they farmers, cheese makers, anglers or market people—are committed to excellence. They recognize the benefits of the climate and the countryside untouched by industrialization, and they see that Irish produce has unrivaled natural goodness and variety.

In this book we have created a variety of recipes that not only highlight Ireland's tremendous products, but also emphasize our tastes and background. There are a few of our favorite Irish dishes, but the majority are simply modern, exciting preparations that reflect our training in London and North America, and our travels throughout Asia, India, and China. Our experiences led toward honest food, simple and pure flavors, letting the ingredients speak out. Regardless of what country or cuisine it was, the best meals, the lingering memories, all had one common thread, and that was the quality of the ingredients.

Out trip around Ireland, and the many interesting characters whom we met, will remain with us the rest of our lives.

Paul and Jeanne Rankin

CHAPTER ONE

The Cheese Maker

One would imagine that with such a wealth of lush, pure pastures, Ireland would also have a great tradition of cheese making. In actual fact, it is really only in the last fifteen years that Irish cheese makers have come into their own. From barely a dozen in production in the early 1980s, there are now over 170 varieties to choose from. Can any other product boast of such a fantastic revival?

One might logically ask why this has happened. The renaissance of the cottage industry scene in general has probably been one of the biggest factors. More and more Europeans have settled in Ireland in the last decade, opting for a quieter country lifestyle that they can no longer find in their homelands (compared to parts of Europe, Ireland is still underdeveloped and underpopulated). These immigrants bring with them their crafts as well as their tastes. As people travel abroad more, they return with more liberated ideas toward different foods, different tastes. They've learned that there's more to cheese than Cheddar. And, of course, the tourist industry is always there, loving all things made in Ireland.

Flavor and variety begin with the type of milk: cows', sheep's, or goats'. It can also be influenced by the animals' diet: green meadows, wild flowers, sparse heather and gorse, and so on. From the separating of the curds, the options are dealt by the cheese maker: how he or she cuts the curd, salts it, molds it, and, of course, how and where he or she matures the cheeses. It is wonderful to be so spoiled by such an array of types, tastes, and textures!

A great number of these Irish cheeses, far too numerous to list, have attained international recognition, and with the Irish Farmhouse Cheese-makers Guild (CAIS) representing and helping to promote them, the adventurous cheese maker can only go in one direction—forward.

Just remember that transportation, packaging, and storage can all be damaging to cheese if it's not treated properly throughout these stages. So if you can, try to buy direct. If not—and this is just about as good—find a dependable supplier. You'll be missing out if you don't.

Baked Cheddar and Scallion Soup

THIS HOMESPUN VERSION OF THE CLASSIC FRENCH ONION SOUP IS JUST AS GOOD AS THE ORIGINAL. IF YOU DECIDE TO PUREE THE SOUP BASE IN A FOOD PROCESSOR, IT MAKES ASSEMBLING IT MUCH EASIER: YOU DON'T HAVE TO SLICE THE ONIONS SO FINELY, AND YOU DON'T HAVE TO MAKE THE ROUX SEPARATELY.

Serves 4 to 6 (V)

1 1/2 pounds onions, sliced

4 tablespoons unsalted butter

1 1/2 cups dry white wine

3 tablespoons all-purpose flour

9 cups vegetable or chicken stock

1 Bouquet Garni (see page 188)

salt and freshly ground
white pepper

1 egg yolk

7 tablespoons light cream

2 3/4 cups grated Cheddar cheese
(11 ounces)

1 bunch scallions, thinly sliced

8 to 12 slices day-old baguette,
toasted

Preheat the oven to 400 degrees F.

In a large saucepan, gently sauté the onions in half of the butter without letting them color. Add the wine and continue to cook until the wine has almost evaporated.

Meanwhile, make a light roux by melting the remaining butter in a 2 1/2-quart saucepan. Add the flour and cook gently without coloring for 2 minutes, stirring constantly. Allow the roux to cool slightly, then whisk the stock into the roux until you have a smooth, lightly thickened stock. Add this to the onions with the Bouquet Garni and a little salt. Simmer gently for about 30 minutes. Taste carefully and season with salt and white pepper.

At this point, you may puree the soup in a food processor to make it smooth and thick, or leave it with the onion slices whole.

To serve, place individual ovenproof bowls on a baking sheet. In a small bowl, whisk together the egg yolk and cream and add 2 tablespoons of this liaison to each bowl. Sprinkle half of the cheese and half of the scallions on top. Ladle in the hot soup and float 2 slices of baguette on each serving. Top with the remaining scallions and cheese. Bake in the preheated oven for at least 5 minutes, or until the tops are bubbling and crusty brown. Serve at once.

Peppery Pizzas
with Ardrahan Cheese

EVERYONE LOVES PIZZA AND THIS IS A PERSONAL FAVORITE. NICE AND SPICY, FRESH AND NATURAL, IT'S JUST THE TICKET TO SATISFY SERIOUS PIZZA CRAVINGS. USE ANY COMPLEMENTARY CHEESE, ALTHOUGH NEVER THE FAKE PROCESSED STUFF. ARDRAHAN CHEESE COMES FROM COUNTY CORK AND IS MADE FROM PASTEURIZED COWS' MILK. IT IS SIMILAR TO DANISH HAVARTI. **Makes 6 individual pizzas** Ⓥ

Prepare the pizza bases as directed.

Preheat the oven to 400 degrees F.

To make the sauce, in a sauté pan, gently sauté the onion and garlic in the oil over medium heat until they are soft and translucent. Add the bell peppers, tomatoes, and tomato paste. Cover and cook over medium-low heat for about 20 minutes. Season with salt and pepper.

Meanwhile, prepare the toppings: Sauté the oyster or button mushrooms in a sauté pan over high heat in 1 tablespoon of the olive oil until soft. Season with salt and pepper and transfer to a platter. Gently fry the chili peppers in the same pan in 1 tablespoon of the olive oil until soft. Season with salt and pepper and transfer to the platter. Then fry the onions in the remaining 2 tablespoons oil until soft but not browned. Set aside.

Pick the cilantro leaves off the bunch and chop them roughly. Set aside. Slice the cheese into fairly thin slices; if sliced too thick, it won't melt properly.

Spread some of the sauce onto each pizza base (which will be cooled or nearly so). Divide the toppings evenly among the 6 bases. Bake in the preheated oven for about 5 minutes or until the cheese is melted and bubbly and starting to brown. Serve at once.

For the bases:

**6 Gourmet Pizza bases
(see page 179)**

For the sauce:

1 small onion, finely chopped

1 garlic clove

2 tablespoons olive oil

2 red bell peppers, seeded and sliced

3 ripe tomatoes, peeled, seeded, and roughly chopped

1 tablespoon tomato paste

salt and freshly ground black pepper

For the toppings:

1 pound fresh oyster mushrooms or button mushrooms, trimmed

4 tablespoons olive oil

salt and freshly ground black pepper

3 fresh chili peppers, mild or hot as preferred, seeded and sliced

2 red onions, sliced

1 bunch fresh cilantro

1 pound Ardrahan or other cheese

OVERLEAF:
Left: Baked Goats' Cheese with Roasted Beets (page 16)

Right: Lemon-Scented Cheese and Berry Tartlets (page 20)

Baked Goats' Cheese
with Roasted Beets

SOME MARRIAGES SEEM MADE IN HEAVEN, AND THIS ONE CERTAINLY IS. EACH FLAVOR IS STRONG ENOUGH TO BALANCE THE OTHER YET STILL REMAINS DISTINCT. THE DISH HAS NICE TEXTURE CONTRASTS, TOO. CHOOSE A FIRM GOATS' CHEESE THAT WILL NOT COLLAPSE IN THE HEAT OF THE OVEN. **Serves 4** (V)

1 pound baby beets

1 pound semi-aged goats' cheese

1 tablespoon walnut oil

2/3 cup homemade coarse dried bread crumbs

a few mixed salad leaves such as arugula, frisée, or romaine

2/3 cup walnuts, lightly toasted

For the walnut vinaigrette:

1 teaspoon Dijon mustard

salt and freshly ground black pepper

2 tablespoons white wine vinegar

4 tablespoons peanut or sunflower oil

4 tablespoons walnut oil

To prepare the vinaigrette, in a small bowl, dissolve the mustard and a dash of salt and pepper in the wine vinegar. Whisk or stir in the oils. Taste for seasoning and adjust the salt and pepper if necessary. Set aside to blend the flavors.

Preheat the oven to 325 degrees F.

Trim each beet, but do not peel. Wrap them individually in aluminum foil and place in the preheated oven. Roast for about 1 hour, or until tender when pierced. Remove from the oven and allow to cool. Peel the beets carefully, then cut into 1/4-inch-thick slices. Place the slices in a bowl and toss with just enough of the vinaigrette to coat.

Increase the oven temperature to 375 degrees F.

Peel the goats' cheese of any rind and slice into 3/4-inch-thick rounds. Brush the slices with the walnut oil, then coat evenly on all surfaces with the bread crumbs. Bake in the preheated oven for about 10 minutes, or until the cheese is heated through and melting at the edges.

Dress the salad leaves with the walnut vinaigrette and arrange in the center of 4 plates. Place the toasted goats' cheese rounds on top. Arrange several beet slices around the salads and drizzle with a little of the remaining vinaigrette. Garnish with the walnuts, sprinkling around and over the salad greens and beets. Serve at once.

Wilted Cabbage Salad
with Bacon and Cashel Blue Cheese

A WARM, WINTERY SALAD WITH SAVORY FLAVORS THAT ENTICE AND WIN OVER EVEN THOSE WHO THINK THEY DON'T LIKE CABBAGE. YOU CAN USE ANY FAVORITE BLUE CHEESE—STILTON, ROQUEFORT—IN PLACE OF THE TRADITIONAL IRISH CASHEL. **Serves 6**

Preheat the oven to 350 degrees F.

To make the croutons, toss the bread cubes in 2 tablespoons of duck or goose fat and spread on a baking sheet. Bake in the preheated oven for about 10 minutes, tossing and turning frequently until they are golden brown and crusty. Remove from the oven and set aside.

To make the dressing, sauté the bacon pieces in 2 tablespoons of duck or goose fat in a large frying pan over medium heat until the bacon is beginning to crisp nicely. Remove the bacon with a slotted spoon to a plate.

Add the garlic to the same pan and fry it gently for 1 minute. Remove from the heat and carefully add the wine vinegar. Scrape the bottom of the pan to loosen any caramelized juices. Taste the hot dressing for salt and add some pepper.

To wilt the cabbage, heat a very large frying pan with the remaining 2 tablespoons duck or goose fat over medium heat. Add the cabbage all at once. Cook, stirring, for about 1 1/2 minutes, or until the cabbage has wilted. Tip into a large bowl.

To serve, add the radicchio, bacon, cheese, and croutons to the warm cabbage and toss with the dressing of wine vinegar and juices. Spoon some of the cabbage mixture into a biscuit cutter or cooking ring 4 inches in diameter and press down slightly until the cabbage mixture forms a neat shape. Carefully remove the ring. Repeat with all the cabbage mixture and arrange the molded cabbage rounds on warmed plates. Serve at once.

3 slices white bread, cut into 1/2-inch cubes

6 tablespoons rendered duck or goose fat

7 ounces bacon, cut into 2-inch pieces

1 garlic clove, chopped

3 tablespoons red wine vinegar

salt and freshly ground black pepper

1 head Savoy cabbage, thick stalks removed and leaves sliced

1/2 head radicchio, thinly sliced

7 ounces Cashel or other blue cheese, crumbled

Dark Chocolate Cheesecake
with Raspberry Coulis

EVERYONE SHOULD HAVE A GOOD CHEESECAKE RECIPE. IT KEEPS WELL, CAN BE MADE A COUPLE OF DAYS IN ADVANCE, AND IS ALWAYS A REAL CROWD PLEASER! THE QUANTITIES GIVEN HERE WILL MAKE ABOUT 14 OUNCES OF PRALINE. YOU CAN STORE THE EXTRA IN AN AIRTIGHT CONTAINER FOR A MONTH OR SO. IT IS WONDERFUL SPRINKLED OVER ICE CREAM. WE USUALLY USE A FOOD PROCESSOR FOR THIS RECIPE.

Serves 10 to 12 (V)

For the praline:

scant 2 1/4 cups hazelnuts (11 ounces)

1/2 cup sugar

4 tablespoons water

For the base:

5 ounces hazelnut praline

11 ounces graham crackers

4 tablespoons unsalted butter, melted

For the filling:

2 1/4 pounds cream cheese, at room temperature

4 eggs

3/4 cup plus 2 tablespoons crème fraîche or sour cream

18 ounces semisweet chocolate, melted and cooled

1 tablespoon vanilla extract

4 tablespoons Cognac or rum (optional)

For the coulis:

2 cups (about 8 ounces) raspberries

3/4 cup plus 2 tablespoons Sugar Syrup (see page 187)

juice of 1 lemon

Preheat the oven to 350 degrees F. Grease a baking sheet with a rim.

To make the praline, place the hazelnuts on a baking sheet. Toast in the preheated oven for about 10 minutes, or until the skins are dark but not black and are beginning to loosen. Remove from the oven and, while the nuts are still warm, wrap them in a kitchen towel and rub vigorously between your palms to loosen the skins. Nearly all the skins should be flaked off, and the hazelnuts should be a golden brown.

Place the sugar and water in a heavy-bottomed pan and stir over low heat until the sugar has dissolved. Continue to cook over high heat, brushing down the sides of the pan as the sugar cooks to avoid crystallization. This can be done with a pastry brush dipped in water. When the caramel is medium brown, it is ready.

Spread the hazelnuts on the prepared baking sheet in a single layer. Pour the caramel carefully over the nuts, trying to coat all of them. Use a spatula to fold the caramel and nuts over to ensure the caramel is evenly distributed. Leave to cool. Break into smallish pieces, then crush or pulse in a food processor until coarsely ground.

Reduce the oven temperature to 325 degrees F. Butter a 9- or 10-inch springform cake pan.

To make the base, weigh out the praline and crush or process in a food processor until medium fine. Pour into a bowl. Crush or process the crackers in a food processor until very fine, then add to the praline. Pour in the melted butter and mix the ingredients together. The mixture should be fairly sticky but not wet.

Press into the prepared cake pan so that the mixture covers the base to a depth of about 1/4 inch. You may not need to use all of the mixture.

To make the filling, using an electric mixer or wooden spoon, beat the cheese until smooth. Add the eggs and mix until just combined. Add the crème fraîche or sour cream, chocolate, vanilla extract, and the Cognac or rum, if using, and mix until combined, wiping down the sides once or twice if you are using a processor to ensure there are no lumps. Gently pour into the cake pan. Bake for 1 to 1 1/4 hours, or until the whole top of the cheesecake looks set and does not wobble. Transfer to a rack to cool.

To make the coulis, place the raspberries, sugar syrup, and lemon juice in a blender and process until well blended. Rub through a fine-mesh sieve to remove all the seeds. Taste and, if necessary, adjust by adding either a little more sugar syrup or lemon juice. (This sauce can be frozen or kept in the refrigerator for several days.)

To serve, release the pan sides and slide the cake onto a serving plate. To ensure a smooth cut, slice the cake using a knife that has been dipped into hot water and quickly dried. Carefully, with a palette knife, place the pieces on chilled plates and surround them with the raspberry coulis. If desired, top the cheesecake with a sprinkling of hazelnut praline.

Lemon-Scented Cheese and Berry Tartlets

THE LIGHT, LEMONY CHEESE MIXTURE IS CREAMY AND TANGY AND IS A PERFECT BALANCE FOR THE SWEET BERRIES. CHOOSE RIPE, UNBRUISED BERRIES; WHATEVER IS IN SEASON WILL ALWAYS TASTE BEST.

Serves 4 (V)

9 ounces Sweet Shortcrust Pastry (see page 184)

1 egg yolk, lightly beaten

For the filling:

8 ounces cream cheese, at room temperature

2/3 cup sour cream

1 egg

7 tablespoons superfine sugar

3/4 teaspoon vanilla extract

finely grated zest and juice of 1/2 lemon

3 1/2 cups (about 14 ounces) mixed berries such as raspberries, blackberries, blueberries, and strawberries, in any combination

confectioners' sugar for sprinkling

whipped cream and/or Raspberry Coulis (see page 18)

Preheat the oven to 350 degrees F. Lightly butter four 4-inch tartlet pans.

To prepare tartlet shells, on a lightly floured board, roll out the pastry 1/8 inch thick. Cut out rounds to fit the tartlet pans, and fit the rounds in the prepared pans, trimming the edges. Place in the refrigerator to chill for at least 20 minutes.

Line the pastry-lined pans with parchment paper (or aluminum foil) and fill with pie weights or dried beans. Bake blind in the preheated oven for about 10 minutes, or until golden brown. Remove the weights or beans and the paper and brush the insides lightly with the egg yolk. Set aside on a rack to cool.

Reduce the oven temperature to 300 degrees F.

To make the filling, whisk together all the filling ingredients either with an electric mixer or by hand until smooth and homogenous. Taste for flavor. Depending on the lemon, you may want to add slightly more lemon juice or slightly more sugar. You do want the filling to be nice and tart to balance the natural sweetness of the berries.

Spoon the filling into the prebaked tartlet pans, taking care not to spill any over the edges of the pastry. Place in the preheated oven to bake for just 8 minutes. The filling should still be wobbly in the center when you remove the tartlets from the oven. (Remember, they will continue to cook even after being removed from the oven). Let cool on a rack.

When the tartlets are cool, remove them from the pans. Carefully heap a pile of the berries in a generous fashion on top of the fillings. A sprinkling of confectioners' sugar over the berries adds an attractive finish. Serve with a dollop of whipped cream or with Raspberry Coulis, or both.

CHAPTER TWO

The Smokery

Smoking has long been a traditional method of food preservation. Here in Ireland, there is a great history of smokehouses, and there is still a healthy demand for the finished products. Meat, poultry, and fish would first be salted, either by dry salting or by being immersed in a salty solution called brine. The length of time the product is cured in this way varies greatly, but generally there is a trend for a lighter hand these days, now that it is more of a sought-after flavor as opposed to a vital preserving technique. This curing and the length of time of the actual smoking both contribute richly to the flavor and texture of the finished product.

Fish must be the most commonly smoked food in Ireland. Indeed, her best-known specialty food is smoked salmon. Appreciated as a gourmet product throughout North America, Europe, and Scandinavia, its exquisite flavor and melting texture raise it to a well-deserved pedestal. However, do not underestimate some of the other fish that lend themselves to smoking. Smoked eel, thoroughly undervalued in Britain and Ireland, is considered a gourmet's delight in Europe. Then there is haddock, cod, trout, and, of course, who hasn't heard of kippers, a type of smoked herring.

Nowadays, smoked chicken and pheasant are becoming very popular, as are smoked beef, pork, and more recently, cheese.

Traditionally, oak is the favorite wood to use in the smokehouse, but other hardwoods, such as hickory, maple, and cherrywood, are all due to come into their own. Obviously, each imparts a different flavor to the product. Every smokehouse has its own personal favorite, just as each has its own exacting formula. Some claim the secret is in the brine, others, the type of wood, and still others, the length of smoking time or a combination of these factors.

To our minds, the most important criterion is to start with a good, fresh product. An inferior one will only be masked, not improved upon, by the techniques involved. Thankfully, the use of dyes as a method of lending color to the product is fast becoming unpopular and is dying out. We would doubt anything that turned our fingers yellow or orange as we worked with it.

Smoked foods can be eaten at any stage of a meal. There are no hard-and-fast rules. Just follow your own taste buds.

Celery Root Soup
with Smoked Pheasant

THIS HEARTY SOUP IS SIMPLE, YET SOUNDS QUITE GLAMOROUS. IF YOU CAN'T FIND SMOKED PHEASANT, USE SOME SMOKED HAM, OR EVEN BACON. **Serves 6 to 8**

In a large pot, gently sauté the onions in the butter over medium heat for about 10 minutes, or until they are just starting to color. Add the celery root, the smoked pheasant, bay leaf, water, and salt to taste. Bring to a boil, and skim off any scum that rises to the surface. Turn the heat down to low, and simmer gently for 30 minutes.

Remove from the heat and take out the pheasant carcass, the drumsticks, and the bay leaf. Discard the bay leaf. After the carcass has cooled, pry off small pieces of meat. Take all the meat off the drumsticks as well, chop roughly, and reserve.

Working in batches, puree the soup in a blender to a smooth consistency, and adjust the seasoning with salt and pepper.

Place a little pheasant meat in the bottom of each warmed soup bowl and ladle the soup on top. Garnish with a swirl of the lightly whipped cream, if desired, and sprinkle with parsley.

2 medium onions, sliced

4 tablespoons unsalted butter

1 celery root (celeriac), peeled and cut into 3/4-inch dice

1 smoked pheasant carcass, plus drumsticks

1 bay leaf

9 cups water

salt and freshly ground white pepper

4 tablespoons whipping cream, lightly whipped (optional)

2 tablespoons chopped fresh parsley

Smoked Pheasant Salad
with Creamed Lentils and Roasted Garlic

SMOKED POULTRY IS AN EXCELLENT AND VERSATILE PRODUCT. TRY THIS SALAD WITH SMOKED CHICKEN, DUCK, OR TURKEY. KEEP ANY BONES FOR MAKING STOCK, AND USE THE STOCK FOR YOUR NEXT BATCH OF CELERY OR LENTIL SOUP. **Serves 4**

1 whole garlic bulb

3/4 cup plus 2 tablespoons olive oil

2/3 cup dried green lentils

2 1/2 cups water

2 tablespoons chopped carrot

2 tablespoons chopped leek

2 tablespoons chopped onion

1 fresh parsley sprig

1 1/2 teaspoons dried thyme

2 1/2 cups light cream

1 smoked pheasant

salt and freshly ground
black pepper

3/4 cup plus 2 tablespoons
Vinaigrette Dressing (see page 177)

mixed salad greens to serve 4

2/3 cup diced cooked green beans

Preheat the oven to 250 degrees F.

To separate the garlic cloves, put the bulb in a pot of cold water to cover, bring to a boil, and simmer for 5 minutes. Refresh under cold water. Peel the cloves and place in a small ovenproof dish. Roast in the preheated oven for 1 hour.

Meanwhile, place the lentils and water in a large pan, bring to a boil, and simmer for 5 minutes, skimming the scum that comes to the surface. Add the carrot, leek, onion, parsley, and thyme and simmer for 20 minutes, or until tender.

Drain the lentils and place in a bowl. Add the cream and 3 of the roasted garlic cloves. Mix well and keep warm.

Cut the meat off the smoked pheasant carcass. Slice the breast meat thinly and dice the leg meat. Arrange the meat on a baking sheet and season with salt and pepper and a little of the vinaigrette. Pop the pheasant into the preheated oven to warm slightly.

Toss the salad greens lightly in the remaining vinaigrette and arrange in the center of the plate. Spoon some of the creamed lentils around the salad and sprinkle on the diced green beans and the remaining roasted garlic. Arrange the pheasant attractively on top of the salad. Serve while the lentils and pheasant are still warm.

Cod Fillet
with Smoked Garlic and Parsley Butter

PERKING UP SAUCES OR SOUPS WITH LITTLE SCRAPS OF SMOKED FISH OR MEAT ADDS A WONDERFUL SAVORY TANG AND DEPTH OF FLAVOR, SO DON'T THROW OUT THOSE TRIMMINGS. FREEZE THEM TO USE IN YOUR NEXT DINNER PARTY DISH. **Serves 4**

To make the parsley butter, melt the butter in a small pan with the smoked salmon trimmings (use the lean pieces from the smoky outside trim of the salmon) and crushed garlic. Cook gently for about 10 minutes, or until the butter has clarified. Allow the butter to rest off the heat for 30 minutes to allow the flavors to infuse.

Meanwhile, pick the parsley leaves off the stems and blanch the leaves in boiling water for 1 minute. Refresh under very cold water, drain, and roughly chop with a large knife. Set aside.

Strain the clarified butter through a fine-mesh sieve into a small frying pan or saucepan, add the lemon juice, and season with salt and pepper.

Blanch or steam the vegetables until tender, then refresh them under cold water and set aside.

To cook the cod fillets, season them with salt and pepper, then dredge them in the flour, shaking off the excess. Heat the vegetable oil in a large frying pan until almost smoking and add the butter and the cod fillets. Cook over medium heat for about 4 minutes on each side. Be careful not to treat the fillets roughly or they will tend to break up.

To serve, warm the cooked vegetables and the parsley in the parsley butter. Spoon this mixture onto warmed plates and top with the cod. Serve at once.

4 thick cod fillets, about 7 ounces each

salt and freshly ground white pepper

scant 3/4 cup all-purpose flour

2 tablespoons vegetable oil

knob of unsalted butter

For the parsley butter:

1/2 cup plus 2 tablespoons (5 ounces) unsalted butter

2 ounces smoked salmon trimmings

3 garlic cloves, crushed

1 small bunch fresh parsley

3 tablespoons fresh lemon juice

salt and freshly ground black pepper

For the vegetables:

5 ounces carrots, peeled and diced

5 ounces leeks, well rinsed and diced

5 ounces potatoes, peeled and diced

OVERLEAF:
Left: Smoked Pheasant Salad with Creamed Lentils and Roasted Garlic (page 24)
Right: Smoked Salmon and Whole-Wheat Bread Millefeuille with Marinated Red Onion (page 30)

Smoked Haddock Tartlets
with Watercress and Mustard Hollandaise

PAUL GREW UP EATING SMOKED HADDOCK AND HAS ALWAYS LOVED IT. IN RECENT YEARS, WE'VE NOTICED IT ON A FEW FANCY PARIS MENUS, WHICH IS GREAT AND JUST REMINDS US NOT TO TAKE THE SIMPLE THINGS FOR GRANTED. PUFF PASTRY ALSO WORKS WELL WITH THIS RECIPE. **Serves 4**

1/3 recipe Savory Shortcrust Pastry (see page 181)

1 1/2 pounds naturally smoked haddock

1 1/4 cups milk

salt

1 bunch watercress

2 tablespoons unsalted butter

For the hollandaise sauce:

3 egg yolks

1 teaspoon water

1 cup plus 2 tablespoons (9 ounces) unsalted butter, chilled and finely diced

1 teaspoon fresh lemon juice

1 tablespoon hot Dijon mustard

salt and freshly ground white pepper

Preheat the oven to 400 degrees F. Lightly butter four 4-inch tartlet pans.

To prepare the tartlet shells, on a lightly floured board, roll out the pastry 1/8-inch thick. Cut out rounds to fit the tartlet pans, and fit the rounds in the prepared pans, trimming the edges. Line the pastry-lined pans with parchment paper (or aluminum foil) and fill with pie weights or dried beans. Bake blind in the preheated oven for 10 to 15 minutes, or until cooked and golden brown. Remove the weights or beans and the paper. Set aside on a rack to cool. Leave the oven temperature set at 400 degrees F.

To make the hollandaise, place the yolks and water in the top pan of a double boiler and place over the lower pan of simmering water (or use a nonreactive saucepan and a bain-marie). Whisk until the egg yolks are smooth and thick. Whisk in the cold, diced butter, a spoonful at a time, until all the butter has been absorbed and the sauce looks thick and creamy. Season with lemon juice, mustard, salt, and pepper. Leave to stand over a pan of warm water; the sauce must not be allowed to get too hot.

Trim the haddock fillets, carefully removing all the bones. Pour the milk into a wide pan and bring to a simmer. The milk needs to be seasoned with salt, but the amount really depends on how salty the smoked fillets are, as the saltiness varies depending on the source of the product. Place the fillets in the milk, lightly cover with parchment paper, and poach for 3 to 4 minutes. Allow them to cool in the milk. When they are cool enough to handle, peel off the skin and break the haddock flesh into large flakes onto a microwave-safe plate or a heatproof dish. Set aside.

Pick through the watercress, removing the stems and any yellow leaves. Rinse well, then drop into boiling salted water. Drain immediately and cool quickly under cold water. Squeeze gently until the watercress is almost dry and place it on the plate with the haddock. Dot the watercress with the butter and then cover with plastic wrap if using a microwave or aluminum foil if heating over water.

Reheat the fish and watercress in the microwave for 1 minute on High, or for about 5 minutes over a pan of simmering water.

Warm the tartlet bases in the oven. Spoon the watercress evenly into the tartlet bases, top with the smoked haddock, and then a generous dollop of hollandaise. Serve immediately.

Warm Pasta Salad
with Smoked Salmon and Fresh Herbs

THIS IS A BEAUTIFUL, LIGHT DISH FOR A SUMMER LUNCH. ONCE YOU BECOME FAMILIAR WITH IT, BE CREATIVE, CHANGING BOTH THE PASTA TYPE AND THE GARNISHES TO SUIT YOUR MOOD. **Serves 6**

In a large pot, bring plenty of water to a rolling boil. Add the pasta and cook until al dente. Drain the pasta and place in a large serving bowl. Add the olive oil, sour cream, lemon juice, and plenty of salt and pepper, and toss well.

Allow to cool slightly for 5 minutes, then add the lettuce, smoked salmon, and the herbs. Toss gently and serve immediately.

1 pound dried short pasta such as conchiglie, penne, or fusilli

2/3 cup light olive oil

2/3 cup sour cream

3 tablespoons fresh lemon juice

salt and freshly ground white pepper

5 ounces romaine lettuce, shredded

9 ounces smoked salmon, thinly sliced and cut into 1/2-inch squares

2 tablespoons finely snipped fresh chives

1 tablespoon roughly chopped fresh dill

Smoked Salmon and Whole-Wheat Bread Millefeuille
with Marinated Red Onion

SMOKED SALMON AND WHOLE-WHEAT BREAD ARE CONSUMED TOGETHER IN VAST QUANTITIES ALL OVER
IRELAND. THIS IS OUR VERSION OF THAT PAIRING, WHICH IS REALLY JUST A FANCY DOUBLE-DECKER SANDWICH.
A COARSE, STONE-GROUND WHOLE WHEAT IS THE BEST BREAD TO USE. IF MUSTARD CRESS IS NOT AVAILABLE,
USE PEPPER CRESS, ALFALFA SPROUTS, OR OTHER TENDER SPROUTS. **Serves 4**

1 red onion, finely chopped

1 tablespoon rice wine vinegar

**1 tablespoon Sugar Syrup
(see page 187)**

7 ounces whole-wheat bread

11 ounces smoked salmon

2 ounces cream cheese

2 tablespoons crème fraîche

**1 small bunch fresh chives,
finely snipped**

3 tablespoons whipping cream

juice of 1/4 lemon

salt

1 bunch mustard cress

**1/2 cucumber, peeled,
seeded, and thinly sliced**

4 radishes, thinly sliced

a few mixed salad leaves

**1 1/2 tablespoons extra-virgin
olive oil**

In a small bowl, combine the onion, rice wine vinegar, and syrup and let
stand for 5 to 10 minutes, then drain.

Meanwhile, cut the bread into 12 square slices each 1/4 inch thick. Slice
the smoked salmon into 8 squares of the same size.

Mix together the cream cheese and crème fraîche. Spread each slice
of bread with the cheese mixture, dividing it evenly. Lay the slices of
smoked salmon on top of 8 slices of the bread. Sprinkle the 8 slices
with the marinated chopped onion.

Start to build 4 millefeuille: Place 4 salmon-topped bread slices on
a work surface and top with 4 more salmon-topped bread slices. Place
a cheese-topped bread slice on top of each one and sprinkle with the
chives.

To make the dressing, mix the cream with the lemon juice and salt
to taste.

Place the millefeuilles on individual plates. Arrange around them the
mustard cress, cucumber, radishes, and salad leaves. Drizzle with the
cream dressing and the olive oil. Serve at once.

CHAPTER THREE

The River

Ireland is crisscrossed with a lattice of rivers. They start up in the rugged regions of inland hills and mountains and work their way through the countryside to the many lakes and the coastal waters.

Fed both by springs and frequent rains, these rivers are host to a variety of fish. The two most commonly sought after are the salmon and the trout. As a country relatively undisturbed by the ravages of modern industry, Ireland offers up some of the very best salmon fishing rivers in Europe. The most prolific of these is the Moy in County Mayo. Others nearby are also prosperous: the Easky and the Palmerston, the Newport and the Ballisodare, to mention just a few. Indeed, there are few areas in the world today where there is such a wealth of angling rivers so close together, offering such diversity and promise. For trout, it is usually the Nenagh and the Ollatrim in County Tipperary that come to mind, or the Nore in County Laios. There are far too many, in fact, to try to list here, but just speak to any angling enthusiast and without a doubt, Ireland's rivers and their bounty will come up in conversation.

The salmon must be the most universally esteemed and highly regarded of fish. It is truly a gourmet food, loved for its delicate flavor and firm flesh. It is certainly one of the most versatile fish. It can be served grilled or poached, whole or in steaks or fillets. It makes wonderful mousses, lends itself to pastas, quiches, fish cakes, and salads, and salmon mayonnaise must be one of the most delightful sandwich fillers. It is good hot or cold, but just remember to let its exquisite flavor speak for itself, which is to say, don't overpower it with strong ingredients.

We think most would agree that trout, brown trout in particular, is at its best when it is simply cooked: a simple fry with a little butter and a squeeze of lemon. But this does not mean that it doesn't lend itself to other flavors. Baked and stuffed, cooked en papillote, grilled, or potted, there are many classic methods for cooking this tasty fish.

So even if you are not an eager angler, don't let that stop you from enjoying some of these recipes, all of which keep clean, simple flavors in mind, ones that will let these two fish really speak for themselves.

Marinated Salmon Salad
with Lime and Pickled Ginger

AN ASIAN VERSION OF CEVICHE, PREPARED WITH SALMON, THIS DISH IS LIGHT YET VERY SATISFYING AND COULD BE SERVED AS A SUMMER MAIN COURSE. **Serves 4**

To marinate the salmon, trim the fresh salmon fillet very well, cutting away any brown parts and making sure there are no bones. Slice the fillet into about 16 thin slices and lay these in a ceramic or stainless-steel dish.

Whisk the lime juice, salt, and sugar together in a small bowl, then pour it over the salmon pieces. Allow this to marinate for 5 to 10 minutes, depending on how "cooked" you prefer your salmon. The longer it marinates, the less raw the salmon will look. It will turn lighter, a result of the marinade "cooking" the fish.

To make the vinaigrette, combine all the ingredients except the oils together in a bowl and whisk until the salt has dissolved. Slowly whisk in the oils, a drop at a time, and taste for seasoning. This vinaigrette will not emulsify completely.

To serve, toss together the lettuce, cilantro, and pickled ginger with a little of the vinaigrette. Divide among individual plates, arranging neatly by pressing the salad into a biscuit cutter or cooking ring 4 inches in diameter. Drain the salmon slices and place on top of the salad. Garnish each serving with a little rosette of pickled ginger and a sprig of fresh cilantro.

1 pound fresh salmon fillet

juice of 3 limes

1 teaspoon salt

2 teaspoons superfine sugar

2 heads Little Gem lettuce or other favorite lettuce, sliced

2 tablespoons chopped fresh cilantro

2 tablespoons thinly sliced pickled ginger, preferably Japanese

For the sesame-ginger vinaigrette:

2 tablespoons finely grated ginger root

4 tablespoons rice wine vinegar

2 tablespoons dark soy sauce

salt and freshly ground white pepper

7 tablespoons Asian sesame oil

7 tablespoons vegetable oil

To garnish:

sliced pickled ginger

a few fresh cilantro sprigs

Salmon Appetizers

THIS IS REALLY THREE DISHES MASQUERADING AS ONE. EACH IS SUFFICIENTLY GOOD TO STAND UP BY ITSELF, BUT TOGETHER, WITH A LIGHT HAND, THEY BECOME A LUXURIOUS EXTRAVAGANZA! **Serves 6**

For the salmon and shrimp sausage:

11 ounces fresh salmon fillet

1 egg white

2/3 cup whipping cream

salt and freshly ground white pepper

5 ounces fresh-cooked shrimp meat

1 tablespoon finely snipped fresh chives

1 tablespoon chopped fresh parsley

For the smoked salmon:

6 thin slices smoked salmon, about 1 ounce each

a few mixed salad leaves

2 tablespoons Vinaigrette Dressing (see page 177)

For the salmon, avocado, and sun-dried tomato vinaigrette:

12 ounces fresh salmon fillet

6 oil-packed sun-dried tomatoes

1/2 cup Vinaigrette Dressing (see page 177)

1 avocado

juice of 1/2 lemon

salt and freshly ground white pepper

1 tablespoon vegetable oil

To make the sausage, cut the salmon into 1/4-inch dice with a sharp knife. Reserve half in a small bowl. Chill the other half and chill a bowl or a food processor bowl. Put the chilled salmon in the chilled bowl with the egg white. If the ingredients are not cold, the mousse will separate when the cream is added. Blend the ingredients together or pulse in the food processor until very smooth. Add the cream and salt and pepper to taste and blend again until the cream is incorporated. Tip the mousse mixture into a bowl and stir in the reserved diced salmon. Add the shrimp, chives, parsley, and salt and pepper to taste. Mix together well.

To form the sausages, place a 12-by-18-inch sheet of plastic wrap on a work surface. Spoon half of the filling onto one end of the plastic wrap and form into a large sausage shape. Pull the wrap over the sausage and twist both ends to seal and tighten the sausage. Repeat with the other half of the mixture.

To cook the sausages, place them in a steamer basket over boiling water for 8 minutes (or poach them in salted water for 10 minutes). Allow them to cool, then unwrap and cut on a 45-degree angle into slices 1/2 inch thick. Set aside.

To prepare the smoked salmon, cut out any brown parts from the salmon. Shape the slices into neat rosette-type shapes. Break the salad leaves into small pieces and toss in the vinaigrette. Set both the rosettes and the salad aside.

To prepare the vinaigrette, cut the fresh salmon into 6 pieces. Chop the sun-dried tomatoes, then puree them in a blender with the vinaigrette. Pit and peel the avocado, slice into 12 pieces, and toss with the lemon juice.

Season the fresh salmon with salt and white pepper. Heat the vegetable oil in a frying pan over high heat and fry the salmon for just 3 minutes on each side. Remove from the heat.

To assemble the dish, put a little of the tossed salad in the middle of each of the 6 plates and set a rosette of smoked salmon at the top of each plate at 12 o'clock (beside the salad, not on top of it). Spoon some sun-dried tomato vinaigrette onto each plate at 4 o'clock, and arrange a piece of sautéed salmon on top of this. Set 2 slices of avocado in between the smoked salmon and the sautéed salmon. Fan 3 pieces of sausage at 8 o'clock. Finally, on each plate between the smoked salmon and the sausage, spoon a neat dollop of Basil Mayonnaise. Garnish with the herb sprigs and serve.

To garnish:

6 tablespoons Basil Mayonnaise (see page 53)

a few fresh chervil and dill sprigs

Perfect Salmon
with a Simple Sauce

MANY PEOPLE HAVE ASKED US FOR A RECIPE FOR A TASTY SAUCE TO GO WITH FISH. WELL, THIS IS IT. IT'S A BASE SAUCE THAT CAN BE JAZZED UP WITH ANY AMOUNT OF INTERESTING HERBS OR FLAVORINGS. **Serves 6**

1 side of fresh salmon, about 3 pounds, skinned and boned

2 tablespoons vegetable oil

salt and freshly ground white pepper

For the sauce:

1 3/4 cups (7 ounces) unsalted butter, chilled and finely diced

2 shallots, finely chopped

1 cup dry white wine

1/2 cup whipping cream

salt and freshly ground white pepper

To make the sauce, melt a little of the butter and gently fry the shallots over medium heat for about 2 minutes, or until they are soft and translucent. Add the wine, bring to a boil, and boil until reduced to about 4 tablespoons. Pour in the cream and boil again for 1 minute. Lower the heat to low and start to whisk in the remaining butter, a tablespoon at a time. Continue to whisk until all the butter has been incorporated. If the sauce seems too thick, add a little water; if it seems too thin, boil it carefully to reduce slightly (you must be careful if you do this because of the high butter content). Season with salt and white pepper and set aside just near the stove top in a warm but not at all hot place.

Ask your fishmonger for a skinless, boneless side of fresh salmon. You should probably order this at least 4 hours before you plan to pick it up. Check to see if all the small pin bones in the middle of the fish, above the belly, have been removed. If not, remove them yourself with a small pair of pliers. Paul usually trims the meat off the belly and the tail of the salmon (freeze it for a quiche or something), and just uses the thickest sections. This ensures even cooking. Cut the side into 6 even slices.

Heat the vegetable oil over medium heat in a large, heavy frying pan. When hot, season the salmon fillets with salt and pepper and place carefully in the pan. If it is not hot enough, the salmon slices will stick. Cook over medium heat for 4 minutes without moving the slices, then turn them over and cook for another 3 minutes. They should be ready; you can take a peek inside by opening the flesh with a spatula or your fingers. If it is still a little pink, cook for another minute.

Serve on heated plates with just about any vegetable accompaniment you like and a good ladle of the sauce.

Trout Fillets
with Tomato Compote, Chervil, and Olive Oil

MAKE THIS DISH IN LATE SUMMER WHEN WILD TROUT IS IN SEASON, TOMATOES ARE AT THEIR BEST, AND THE CHERVIL IS YOUNG AND FRAGRANT. **Serves 4**

4 whole trout fillets with skin intact, about 6 ounces each

2/3 cup dry white wine

1 teaspoon olive oil

1 teaspoon salt

For the tomato compote:

2 shallots, finely chopped

1/2 garlic clove, finely chopped

2 tablespoons light olive oil

1 teaspoon tomato paste

6 plum tomatoes, peeled, seeded, and coarsely chopped

salt and freshly ground white pepper

For the chervil dressing:

1 small bunch fresh chervil

1/4 teaspoon salt

freshly ground white pepper

juice of 1 lemon

2/3 cup virgin olive oil

To make the tomato compote, in a frying pan, fry the shallots and garlic gently in the olive oil for about 2 minutes, or until translucent. Add the tomato paste, the chopped tomatoes, and a little salt and pepper. Bring to a boil quickly and simmer for 2 minutes. Remove from the heat.

To make the chervil dressing, pick the chervil leaves off their stems, reserve the stems, and coarsely chop the leaves. In a small bowl, mix the salt and some freshly ground white pepper with the lemon juice and then stir in the oil. Finally, stir in the chopped chervil. Set aside.

To cook the trout, carefully trim the trout fillets. If necessary, scale them with a blunt, serrated knife, and try to take out any small bones with a pair of pliers. Rinse the fillets in cold water and drain in a colander.

Place the wine in a wide saucepan with the reserved chervil stems, oil, and salt and bring to a boil. Carefully put the trout fillets into the wine, cover, and simmer very gently for 2 minutes. Remove from the heat and allow to stand for 1 minute before serving.

Spoon the tomato compote onto warmed plates and drizzle each plate with the chervil oil dressing. Using a slotted spatula, quickly lift the trout fillets from the saucepan and place a fillet on each plate. Serve immediately.

OVERLEAF:

Left: Perfect Salmon with a Simple Sauce (page 36)

Right: Trout Fillets with Tomato Compote, Chervil, and Olive Oil (page 37)

Gratin of Trout
with Cucumber Ribbons and Dill

IT'S GOOD TO LEARN THIS SIMPLE LITTLE GRATIN TECHNIQUE, WHICH CAN BE APPLIED TO ANY MEAT OR FISH DISH WITH A CREAM SAUCE. IF YOU DON'T HAVE A BROILER, THE DISH WILL TASTE FINE WITHOUT THAT STEP.

Serves 4

4 whole trout fillets with skin intact, about 7 ounces each

salt and freshly ground white pepper

1 cucumber

2 tablespoons unsalted butter

4 tablespoons water

For the sauce:

4 shallots, thinly sliced

1 cup dry Riesling

1 1/2 cups whipping cream

1 tablespoon Dijon mustard

1 small bunch fresh dill, picked and chopped

To make the sauce, combine the shallots and wine in a small pan and boil over medium-high heat until reduced to about 6 tablespoons of liquid. Add 1 cup of the cream and boil gently until it thickens to a sauce consistency. Strain through a fine-mesh sieve into a clean pan and reserve in a warm place while you prepare the trout.

Carefully trim the trout fillets. If necessary, scale them with a blunt, serrated knife, and try to take out any small bones with a pair of pliers. Rinse the fillets in cold water and drain in a colander. Cut each fillet into 6 diamond-shaped pieces. (Simply cut the fillet across following the angle at the top of the fillet.) Season with salt and white pepper and arrange in a steaming basket. Steam for 2 minutes.

While the fish is steaming, prepare the cucumber ribbons: Peel the cucumber. Now, using the peeler, remove the flesh in long, ribbonlike strips from all sides until you reach the seeds.

Melt the butter in a pan with the water. Add the cucumber ribbons and some salt and white pepper and cook over high heat for about 2 minutes, or until the ribbons are tender but still slightly crunchy.

To complete the dish, preheat the broiler. Bring the sauce back to a boil, then remove from the heat. Whisk in the mustard and dill. Quickly beat the remaining 1/2 cup cream until soft peaks form.

Divide the cucumber ribbons among warmed flameproof plates and spread them out to form a bed for the trout. Arrange the trout pieces on top, alternating each piece skin side up, skin side down, to form a mosaic-like pattern. Fold the whipped cream into the sauce and spoon a generous amount over the trout. Place each plate under the broiler for about 1 minute, or until it browns beautifully. Serve at once.

Summer Salad Roscoff

THIS SALAD IS INSPIRED BY THE FAMOUS *SALADE NIÇOISE*. WE'RE SURE THAT IF THE PEOPLE OF PROVENCE WERE TO SPEND TIME IN IRELAND, THEY WOULD WHOLEHEARTEDLY APPROVE OF OUR SUBSTITUTING SALMON FOR TUNA. **Serves 4**

To cook the salmon, pour the wine, water, and wine vinegar into a wide pan. Add the Bouquet Garni and salt and bring to a boil. Immerse the salmon fillet in the liquid, and simmer very gently for 2 minutes. Remove from the heat, cover, and allow to cool in the poaching liquid.

To prepare the salad, cook the green beans in salted boiling water for 6 minutes, or until tender-crisp, and then drain. Refresh in cold water, and drain again.

To make the dressing, whisk together the Mayonnaise, basil, and anchovies in a small bowl. Thin with the poaching liquid, whisking continuously. Taste for seasoning, and add salt and pepper as needed.

To serve, toss the salad leaves with the vinaigrette, and arrange attractively in the center of each plate. Arrange the cucumber, tomatoes, eggs, and olives around the edges. Remove the salmon from the poaching liquid, and flake carefully onto each plate. Drizzle with some of the dressing.

3/4 cup plus 2 tablespoons dry white wine

3/4 cup plus 2 tablespoons water

2 tablespoons white wine vinegar

1 Bouquet Garni (see page 188)

1 teaspoon salt

1 pound fresh salmon fillet

For the dressing and salad garnishes:

4 to 5 ounces green beans, cut into 3/4-inch lengths

4 tablespoons Mayonnaise (see page 177)

1 tablespoon chopped fresh basil

2 anchovy fillets, finely minced

2 tablespoons poaching liquid

salt and freshly ground black pepper

4 to 5 ounces mixed salad greens

4 tablespoons Vinaigrette Dressing (see page 177)

1/2 cucumber, peeled, quartered lengthwise, and chopped

9 ounces vine-ripened tomatoes, sliced or cut into wedges

4 hard-cooked eggs (cooked for 9 minutes), peeled and quartered

1 cup imported black olives, pitted

The Lake

Ireland has some of the largest inland lakes in Europe. Because the country is relatively underdeveloped and has little heavy industry, these lakes, or loughs, are teeming with fish, and they attract anglers from all over the world. Trout, pike, and eel, so highly esteemed on the Continent for centuries, are in plentiful supply. One gilly (fishing guide) told us the true story of how some Europeans used to come over on fishing holidays and catch so many pike that upon their return home they could sell their catch (at highly inflated prices, nonetheless) and pay for their whole holiday! Thankfully, stricter measures are now in effect to prevent this from happening and ensure that the lakes are not overfished.

All the Irish lake fish are wonderful for eating, even if the general population hasn't yet realized it. The main reason is because the cold waters are so free from pollution, the fish have pure and healthy diets and consequently bear tasty flesh in prime condition. The people who inhabit the lakeshores know this, but still most of the catch is air-freighted abroad to more appreciative markets.

Perch has a firm white flesh with a delicate flavor. Pike is bonier than other fish, but this certainly doesn't detract from the quality or taste. In King Henry VIII's time, pike would fetch more at the market than a lamb or chicken. The culinary reputation of eels is evident everywhere else; the Dutch, Germans, and the Japanese all go mad over them, whether smoked or fresh.

It is certainly high time that people in Britain and Ireland are encouraged to be more daring in their tastes. Perhaps it is the fault of the shops and fishmongers. If they assume there is no market because of past history and therefore do not stock new items, how are people to give it a chance? We must request these delightful fish, for if there is no demand, there will be no supply.

Deep-fried Perch
with Light Tartare Sauce

TONS OF PERCH ARE FLOWN FROM IRELAND TO THE CONTINENT EVERY YEAR WHERE THE FISH ARE CONSUMED IN VAST QUANTITIES. THIS IS A FAVORITE COOKING TECHNIQUE FOR THE SMALL FILLETS THAT PROTECTS THEIR FLAVOR. **Serves 4**

1 pound perch fillets

vegetable oil for deep-frying

salt

4 tablespoons all-purpose flour

1 lemon, cut into wedges

For the batter:

scant 1 cup all-purpose flour

1 tablespoon vegetable oil

3/4 cup plus 2 tablespoons beer or water

salt and freshly ground white pepper

2 egg whites

For the tartare sauce:

1 cup Mayonnaise (see page 177)

1 tablespoon finely chopped gherkins

1 tablespoon finely chopped capers

1 tablespoon finely chopped fresh parsley

4 to 6 tablespoons water (optional)

To make the batter, sift the flour into a large bowl. Add the oil and beer or water and season with salt and white pepper. Whisk the ingredients together until they are just incorporated. Leave the batter to rest for about 1 hour, or it will "shrink" when cooked. After 1 hour, beat the egg whites to a light froth and carefully fold them into the batter.

To make the tartare sauce, simply combine the Mayonnaise with the gherkins, capers, and parsley. Dilute the mixture with the water if you desire a lighter sauce that will spread on the plate.

To cook the perch fillets, preheat the oil in a deep pan or deep-fat fryer to about 350 degrees F, or until a cube of bread turns golden within 1 minute. Season the perch fillets with salt and coat lightly with the flour, shaking off any excess.

Dip the fillets into the batter, then slip them into the hot oil. Cook for about 3 minutes, or until golden brown. Remove from the pan and transfer to paper towels to drain off excess fat.

To serve, spread a little of the tartare sauce onto each individual plate and divide the perch fillets evenly among them. Serve at once with a wedge of lemon.

Japanese-Style Barbecued Eel
with Stir-fried Vegetables

THIS TECHNIQUE IS CALLED *KABAYAKI*, AND IT IS VERY POPULAR IN JAPAN. EEL LENDS ITSELF WELL TO THE *TERIYAKI*-STYLE FLAVORS HERE, AS DO MANY OTHER FOODS, SO TRY THIS RECIPE WITH CHICKEN OR PORK, TOO. **Serves 4**

Boil the soy sauce and mirin together in a small pan until reduced to about 6 tablespoons. Set aside.

Prepare a charcoal fire or preheat the broiler. When nice and hot, place the eel fillets on the grill rack or on a broiler pan, oil them lightly, and grill or broil for about 5 minutes on each side. Then start to baste them with the reduction of *mirin* and soy sauce. Continue to cook for another 10 minutes, turning as necessary and basting frequently, until tender.

Meanwhile, stir-fry the vegetables: Blanch each of the vegetables in a pan of salted boiling water for about 30 seconds, or until they have just about lost that raw crunch. Allow them to drain well.

Heat the vegetable oil in a large wok or deep frying pan until almost smoking. Add the garlic and ginger, stir briefly, and then stir in the vegetables. Stir-fry for about 45 seconds, then season with salt and pepper and the sesame oil.

To serve, arrange the stir-fried vegetables in the center of warmed plates. Place 3 pieces of eel attractively on top of the vegetables. Garnish with cilantro and sesame seeds.

5 tablespoons dark soy sauce

1/2 cup *mirin* (Japanese cooking wine) or sweet sherry

2 eels, skinned, cleaned, filleted, and cut into 3-inch-thick slices

2 tablespoons vegetable oil

For the stir-fried vegetables:

2 celery stalks, sliced on the diagonal

4 to 5 ounces fresh shiitake mushrooms

1 red bell pepper, cut into strips

4 to 5 ounces snow peas

1 head bok choy, cut into 1 1/2-inch pieces

1 tablespoon vegetable oil

1 teaspoon chopped garlic

1 teaspoon chopped fresh ginger root

salt and freshly ground black pepper

1 teaspoon Asian sesame oil

1 small bunch fresh cilantro

2 tablespoons sesame seeds, toasted

Sautéed Pike with Crayfish
and Garlic Vinaigrette

A PIKE FROM A CLEAN, PURE LAKE IS A GREAT FISH TO EAT. IT WILL NOT HAVE THE COARSE TASTE THAT YOU MAY ASSOCIATE WITH RIVER PIKE. IT'S WONDERFUL FOR THIS RECIPE BECAUSE IT HAS ENOUGH FLAVOR TO STAND UP TO THE GARLIC IN THE VINAIGRETTE. OTHER WHITE FISH CAN ALSO BE USED. **Serves 6**

3 pounds live freshwater crayfish

6 pike fillets, about 6 ounces each

salt and freshly ground white pepper

2 tablespoons vegetable oil

2 tablespoons unsalted butter

For the sauce:

reserved crayfish heads

3 tablespoons vegetable oil

2 tablespoons chopped carrot

2 tablespoons chopped onion

2 garlic cloves

1 tablespoon tomato paste

2 tablespoons brandy

1/2 cup dry white wine

4 1/2 cups water

1 1/4 cups whipping cream

For the vinaigrette:

2 plum tomatoes

3/4 cup plus 2 tablespoons Vinaigrette Dressing (see page 177)

1 teaspoon crushed garlic

1 teaspoon chopped fresh tarragon

1 teaspoon chopped fresh parsley

To garnish:

a few fresh tarragon and chervil sprigs

To cook the crayfish, in a large pot bring plenty of salted water to a boil. Wash the crayfish under running water, then plunge them into the boiling water. Let the water return to a boil and simmer for just 30 seconds. Turn off the heat and let the pan stand for 4 minutes. Drain and refresh the crayfish in cold water. Separate the heads from the tails, reserving the heads for the sauce. Peel the tails. Set aside.

To make the sauce, crush the crayfish heads in a large bowl with a wooden spoon. Heat the oil until smoking in a very large pan, toss in the crushed crayfish heads, and fry over high heat for 3 minutes, stirring. Add the chopped vegetables and garlic and cook for another 2 minutes. Add the tomato paste, brandy, and wine and boil until the wine has reduced by half. Add the water, reduce the heat, and simmer for 20 minutes.

Strain the sauce through a fine-mesh sieve into a clean pan, and discard the contents of the sieve. Boil to reduce the sauce until you have about 1 cup of concentrated juices left. Add the cream and boil until the sauce is thick and creamy.

To make the vinaigrette, blanch the tomatoes in a pan of boiling water for 10 seconds. Transfer them immediately to cold water. Peel off the skins, cut in half, and squeeze out the seeds. Carefully cut the flesh into neat 1/2-inch dice.

In a bowl, whisk together the vinaigrette, garlic, and herbs. Finally, stir in the tomato dice.

To cook the pike, remove any bones with a sharp knife and give the fillets a nice shape. Skin the fillets if this has not already been done.

Season with salt and pepper.

Heat the oil in a large, heavy frying pan until it is almost smoking. Add the butter and as it begins to foam, add the fillets. Sauté for about 3 minutes on each side. Press the fillets gently; if they want to flake apart, they are cooked and ready.

To serve, warm the crayfish tails in the vinaigrette in a small pan. Spoon equal quantities of the vinaigrette, crayfish tails, and then the cream sauce onto warmed plates. Carefully place a fillet in the center of each, and garnish with sprigs of tarragon and chervil.

Freshwater Fish Cakes
with Scallions

THIS IS A SUPER RECIPE FOR USING UP BITS AND PIECES OF FISH OR SHELLFISH OF ALL KINDS. SERVE WITH A SIMPLE SALAD. **Serves 4**

1 to 1 1/4 pounds pike, perch, or other white fish fillets

4 scallions, finely chopped

7 tablespoons Mayonnaise (see page 177)

3 cups fresh bread crumbs, soaked in milk and squeezed dry

1 egg, lightly beaten

1 tablespoon chopped fresh parsley

1 tablespoon chopped fresh thyme

salt and cayenne pepper

1/2 cup ground almonds

3 tablespoons vegetable oil

3 tablespoons unsalted butter

1 recipe Mustard Sauce (see page 64)

Check the fillets to make sure all the bones have been removed, then trim away any dark spots. Cut the fillets into thin strips and then into 1/4-inch dice. Place in a bowl. Mix the fish with the scallions, Mayonnaise, 2 cups of the bread crumbs, the egg, parsley, and thyme, and season with salt and cayenne pepper.

Divide the mixture into 12 equal portions and form each portion into a neat patty about 3 1/2 inches in diameter. Mix together the remaining 1 cup bread crumbs and the ground almonds on a flat plate and dredge each fish cake in the mixture, patting to coat evenly with the crumbs.

Heat the oil in a heavy frying pan and add the butter. When it foams, add 6 of the fish cakes. Cover and cook over medium-high heat for about 3 minutes on each side. Using a slotted spatula, transfer the cakes to paper towels to drain. Cook the remaining 6 cakes in the same way.

Transfer to warmed individual plates and pass the Mustard Sauce.

Salad of Smoked Eel
with Beets and Chives

IF YOU ARE UNFAMILIAR WITH TOP-QUALITY SMOKED EEL, IT IS WELL WORTH TRYING. BUY IT WHOLE WITH THE SKIN ON TO ENSURE FRESHNESS. **Serves 4**

Trim the beets, but do not peel. If you have a microwave, wrap the beets in plastic wrap and cook in the microwave on High for about 12 minutes. Allow to rest for about 5 minutes. Unwrap the beets and, using paper towels, simply push the skins off. Otherwise, boil the beets in water to cover generously for 30 to 60 minutes, or until tender; the timing will depend on the size. Push off the skins. Cut the beets into neat 1/4-inch-thick slices.

Whisk the mustard into the vinaigrette and marinate the beet slices with a little salt and white pepper in half the vinaigrette mixture for at least 30 minutes.

To prepare the eel, pull the head back, breaking the backbone off the neck. Pull the head toward the tail to free the skin and pull it off. Now run a small knife down both sides of the backbone. Pry the flesh away from the bone with your fingers, releasing any tricky bits again with your knife. Cut the fillets into 2 1/2-inch pieces and set aside.

In a small bowl, mix together the cream, lemon juice, chives, and a little salt and white pepper.

To serve, toss the salad leaves with some of the remaining vinaigrette and arrange them in the center of each plate. Arrange the beets in 3 piles around the salad and place pieces of smoked eel in between these piles. Drizzle each plate generously with the chive cream.

2 beets

1 tablespoon Dijon mustard

2/3 cup Vinaigrette Dressing (see page 177)

salt and freshly ground white pepper

1 smoked eel, whole with skin on

4 tablespoons whipping cream

1 tablespoon fresh lemon juice

1 small bunch fresh chives, finely snipped

a few mixed salad leaves

The Shoreline

The western seaboard of Ireland must be one of the world's most unpolluted stretches of coastline. All around her coast is truly a region of plenty. Cockles and mussels, oysters, scallops, shrimp, and lobsters—it is a pure and plentiful harvest awaiting anyone that goes in search.

Although Molly Malone has preached about the wonderful cockles and mussels here for years, they are still vastly underrated and underused locally. Trucks arrive from the Continent on a daily basis to take them back by the ton to Spain and France. Obviously, the people there have a taste for these mollusks and perhaps, as more locals visit these countries, they too will develop an appreciation for them. They definitely deserve it.

Thankfully, there is more local interest in some of the other shellfish. Oysters have always enjoyed a great following here. Indeed, there are several festivals throughout Ireland paying homage to these delicacies. The Galway Festival is perhaps the best known. Every September the town is absolutely engulfed by people, there to consume in great quantities the famous local oysters along with plenty of brown bread and Guinness. What could be better?

All around the coast, restaurants have, especially in recent years, taken to serving more crabs, Dublin Bay prawns (large saltwater crayfishlike prawns), and, of course, lobster. Needless to say, simple treatment is all that is necessary if these products are fresh and in season. Boiling Dublin Bay prawns or lobster and serving them with drawn butter can be one of the most satisfying and memorable meals possible.

A simple preparation actually suits most shellfish best. It lets their wonderful flavor speak for itself. However, they all lend themselves to soups and chowders, pastas, rice dishes, puff pastry, pies, salads, and just about anything else one could dream up. Just be sure to start with a fresh product, don't make the usual mistake of over-cooking, and you will undoubtedly come up with a winner of a dish.

Clam Chowder
with Potatoes and Dulse

CHOWDER IS A WONDERFUL, HEARTY SOUP AVAILABLE IN ALMOST EVERY SEASIDE TOWN IN THE UNITED STATES. WE LOVE IT, AND IN IRELAND WE HAVE ALL THE KEY INGREDIENTS, SO DON'T HESITATE TO TRY IT. DULSE IS A TYPE OF SEAWEED THAT IS POPULAR IN IRELAND AS WELL AS SCOTLAND, AND IS HARVESTED ON BOTH SIDES OF THE ATLANTIC. IT IS AVAILABLE IN SPECIALTY-FOOD SHOPS, OR LOOK FOR A SUITABLE SEAWEED IN JAPANESE MARKETS. **Serves 4 to 6**

2 1/4 pounds live clams

1 ounce dried dulse or other dried seaweed

2 tablespoons chopped onion

2 tablespoons chopped leek

2 tablespoons chopped carrot

1 fresh parsley sprig

1 fresh thyme sprig

1 3/4 cups water

3/4 cup dry white wine

1 onion, finely chopped

5 ounces bacon, any rind removed, chopped

2 tablespoons unsalted butter

1 cup fish stock, light chicken stock, or water

2 large potatoes, roughly diced

3/4 cup plus 2 tablespoons whipping cream

1 tablespoon chopped fresh parsley

whipped cream (optional)

To prepare and cook the clams, wash them under cold running water. Finely slice or chop the dulse with a sharp knife and put it into a large pan with the other aromatics: the 2 tablespoons of chopped onion, leek, carrot, and parsley and thyme sprigs. Add the water, bring to a boil, and simmer for 10 minutes to infuse the flavors. Add the wine and return to a boil.

Add the clams, cover, and boil vigorously for 1 to 2 minutes, until the clams open. Drain them into a colander, being sure to catch the cooking liquid in a bowl underneath. This will be used in the chowder. Set the liquid aside while you pull the clams from their shells. Discard the shells and the sprigs of parsley and thyme. Keep the clams and the aromatics and place them in the reserved liquid.

To make the chowder, fry the finely chopped onion and bacon in the 2 tablespoons butter over medium heat in a large pan until soft and translucent. Add the stock or water and bring to a simmer. Add the potatoes and simmer gently until they are cooked.

Remove half of the potato mixture and blend in a blender or food processor, or mash in a bowl. This will give you a thick, creamy soup that will thicken the whole chowder.

In a clean saucepan, combine the 2 potato mixtures; the clams, aromatics, and cooking liquid; and the cream and bring to a simmer. Taste for seasoning. Ladle into warmed bowls and garnish with the parsley and, if desired, a dollop of whipped cream. Serve at once.

Lobster Salad
with Basil Mayonnaise

IF YOU WANT A GOURMET DISH THAT'S EASY AND QUICK TO MAKE, GO NO FURTHER. THIS IS SIMPLICITY ITSELF AND IT LOOKS AND TASTES STUNNING. **Serves 4**

To make the mayonnaise, whisk together the mustard, salt and pepper to taste, and wine vinegar in a bowl until the salt has dissolved. Add the egg yolks and whisk to combine. Then whisk in the oil, very slowly at first, literally drop by drop. As the mayonnaise starts to build up, you can add the oil slightly faster, but always be sure to incorporate each addition fully before adding more. Add the basil and taste for seasoning. Do not add the basil until the last moment before serving because it will lose its color if it is done too far in advance.

To kill the lobster, place it on a board on its back and drive the point of a sharp knife through the mouth, thereby severing the spinal cord. Or pierce with an ice pick.

To cook the lobster, heat a large pan filled with plenty of water to a vigorous boil. Put the lobster in and let it cook for about 14 minutes. Stop the cooking process by plunging the lobster into a pot of ice cold water.

Insert a knife into the lobster at the point where the tail and body are joined and cut toward the tail. The tail meat will now easily pull away from the shell. Discard any organs. Break off the claws and crack the shells with a heavy knife. Remove the meat from the claws, being careful to discard any pieces of shell. Slice up the meat neatly.

To serve, toss the mixed salad leaves in the vinaigrette and pile in the center of each plate. Surround in an attractive manner with the cherry tomatoes, the avocado slices, and finally the lobster meat. Spoon the mayonnaise onto the plate, either in one generous dollop or, if you prefer, drizzle over the lobster and salad. Serve immediately.

1 live lobster, about 1 1/2 pounds

some mixed salad leaves

2 tablespoons Vinaigrette Dressing (see page 177)

6 red cherry tomatoes, halved

6 yellow cherry tomatoes, halved

1 avocado, pitted, peeled, and sliced

For the basil mayonnaise:

1 tablespoon Dijon mustard

salt and freshly ground white pepper

1 tablespoon white wine vinegar

3 egg yolks

2 cups plus 2 tablespoons vegetable oil or light olive oil

1/2 cup chopped fresh basil

OVERLEAF:

Left: Lobster Salad with Basil Mayonnaise (page 53)

Right: Steamed Symphony of Seafood with Saffron Butter Vinaigrettte (page 69)

Crispy Shrimp Spring Rolls
with a Spiced Cilantro Salsa

WE JUST LOVE CHINESE FOOD AND RESPECT THE CHINESE OBSESSION WITH FRESHNESS. FOR THIS RECIPE WE USE LOCAL LIVE SHRIMP, ORGANIC CABBAGE, AND FRESH CILANTRO. RAW SHRIMP WILL GIVE YOU BY FAR THE BEST FLAVOR—AND LIVE ONES ARE EVEN BETTER—BUT IF YOU HAVE TO USE COOKED SHRIMP, CHOOSE THE BEST QUALITY AND OMIT THE COOKING STAGE. **Serves 4**

16 large fresh shrimp

2 tablespoons vegetable oil

1/4 head Savoy cabbage, thinly sliced

4 ounces fresh shiitake mushrooms, thinly sliced

1 teaspoon chopped fresh ginger root

1 garlic clove

1 teaspoon Asian sesame oil

salt and freshly ground white pepper

4 large spring roll wrappers, cut into 4 squares to yield 16 pieces

2 egg yolks for sealing

about 4 1/2 cups vegetable oil for deep-frying

For the salsa:

1 yellow bell pepper, peeled, seeded, and diced

1 red bell pepper, peeled, seeded, and diced

1 tablespoon vegetable oil

2 plum tomatoes, peeled, seeded, and diced

2 tablespoons rice wine vinegar

1 tablespoon sugar

1 tablespoon tomato ketchup

1 tablespoon finely snipped fresh chives

2 tablespoons chopped fresh cilantro

Bring a large pot of salted water to a boil, add the shrimp, and cook for 3 minutes. Refresh them in cold water, and then peel them so that you have only the fleshy tail meat. Chop this into 1/2-inch dice. Set aside.

Heat the vegetable oil in a large frying pan until it is smoking. Add the cabbage, mushrooms, ginger, and garlic. Stir-fry for exactly 1 minute and then tip into a large bowl. Allow to cool and then add the shrimp and sesame oil and season with salt and pepper. Mix well.

Lay a spring roll wrapper in a diamond shape on a work surface. Arrange one-sixteenth of the shrimp mixture on the wrapper in a cylinder. Fold up the bottom corner over the mixture, then pull in the two side corners. Roll up over the top corner and brush the ends very lightly with the egg yolk to seal closed. Repeat with the remaining wrappers and filling. Note that it is important not to let the wrappers dry out before they are filled. Also, do not overfill them.

To make the salsa, in a frying pan fry the peppers in the oil over a gentle heat for 2 minutes. Add the plum tomatoes and fry gently for 1 minute longer. Add the wine vinegar, sugar, and ketchup, and taste for seasoning. Season with salt and pepper, if necessary. Do not add the chives and cilantro until just before serving.

To serve, heat the oil in a large pan to 350 degrees F, or until a cube of bread turns golden within 1 minute. Fry the spring rolls in small batches for about 5 minutes, or until golden brown. Remove with tongs or a slotted spoon to paper towels to drain.

Serve immediately with plenty of the fresh salsa on the side.

Mussels in a Pesto Broth

THESE MUSSELS ARE DELICIOUS SERVED IN SHALLOW BOWLS WITH PASTA OR CRUSTY BREAD, OR ADD A SPLASH OF WHIPPING CREAM FOR AN ELEGANT SOUP. **Serves 4**

Simmer together the wine, water, and onion in a large pot. Meanwhile, clean the mussels by rinsing them in cold water, and pulling away their hairy beards. Add the mussels to the pot, cover, and boil vigorously for 1 minute. Add the tomatoes and black pepper, and boil for 1 more minute, or until all the mussels have opened. Discard any that remain closed.

Drain the mussels into a colander with a bowl underneath to catch the tasty broth. Reserve the broth. As soon as the mussels are cool enough to handle, shell them.

Add the mussels back to the broth, and heat gently. Do not boil or the mussels will toughen. Stir in the pesto and serve immediately.

1 cup dry white wine

7 tablespoons water

3 tablespoons finely chopped onion

3 pounds live mussels

2 ripe tomatoes, peeled, seeded, and roughly chopped

1 teaspoon cracked black pepper

3 to 4 tablespoons Basil Pesto (see pages 116-117)

Gratin of Oysters
with Leeks and Chardonnay

WE PREFER RAW OYSTERS TO COOKED. IT'S HARD TO BEAT PLAIN BUTTERED WHOLE-WHEAT BREAD AND A GLASS OF GUINNESS TO GO WITH THESE BRINY CREATURES. HOWEVER, IF YOU ARE GOING TO COOK THEM, KEEP IT SIMPLE, SUCH AS THIS DISH, AND DON'T OVERCOOK THEM. **Serves 4**

1 tablespoon unsalted butter

salt and cayenne pepper

2 small leeks, carefully rinsed and thinly sliced

1 1/2 cups Chardonnay

10 oysters, removed from their shells and stored in their juices

1 1/2 cups whipping cream

squeeze of lemon juice

snipped fresh chives

puff pastry crescent (optional)

Preheat the broiler.

Heat the butter in a small pan with a little salt and cayenne pepper and sauté the leeks over gentle heat for about 4 minutes, or until tender. Tip the leeks into flameproof serving dishes to form neat beds. Set aside.

Pour half of the Chardonnay into a small pan. Add the juices of the oysters and boil to reduce by two-thirds. Add half of the cream and boil again until it has achieved a rich sauce consistency. Check the seasoning, add a squeeze of lemon juice, and then set aside. Keep warm.

Whip the remaining cream until it is stiff and place in the refrigerator.

To heat the oysters, place the remaining Chardonnay in a small pan with a little salt and bring to a boil. Immediately tip in the oysters, count to 10, and then remove from the heat. Let them continue to poach off the heat for another 30 seconds. Remove the oysters from the liquid and drain in a sieve or on paper towels. Quickly arrange the oysters on top of the leek beds and keep warm. Don't let the oysters get too hot or they will be rubbery.

To serve, bring the cream sauce back to a boil and add the chives to taste. Fold in the whipped cream very roughly with a spoon and then spoon this sauce over the oysters. Slip the plates under the broiler and watch carefully. After 1 to 2 minutes, the cream will have browned beautifully. Top with a puff pastry crescent, if using, and serve immediately.

Chargrilled Scallops
with a Spaghetti Neri and Saffron Cream Sauce

SCALLOPS REALLY SUIT THE CHARCOAL GRILL. IT SEEMS TO BRING OUT THEIR NATURAL SWEETNESS. QUALITY AND FRESHNESS ARE OF THE UTMOST IMPORTANCE, SO DON'T ACCEPT SHELLFISH THAT HAVE BEEN SOAKED IN WATER TO INCREASE THEIR SIZE. **Serves 4**

Prepare a charcoal fire.

Trim the scallops, carefully removing any sand, membrane, and tough muscle and any ragged edges. This trim is used in the sauce, so don't throw it out. Dry the scallops on paper towels.

To make the sauce, fry the shallots, garlic, and scallop trim (or white fish) in the butter over medium heat for about 4 minutes. Do not let it color. Add the wine and the saffron and boil until the wine has reduced to about 3 tablespoons. Add the cream and simmer until the cream has reduced and thickened to sauce consistency. Season with salt and pepper and pass through a fine-mesh sieve into a clean pan. Set aside.

Cook the fresh pasta in a large pan of salted boiling water for about 1 minute, or until all the pasta floats to the surface. Drain the pasta, place in a warmed bowl, and toss with the butter and a little salt and white pepper. Set aside and keep warm.

In a bowl, toss the scallops in the light olive oil with salt and white pepper. Quickly place the scallops on a rack over a very hot charcoal fire (alternatively, use a very hot cast-iron frying pan). Allow them to cook and brown without touching or moving them for the first 2 minutes. Turn them over and cook them for 1 minute on the other side.

To serve, arrange the pasta in the middle of warmed plates. Top with the scallops and pour over and around the saffron cream sauce. Garnish with a few fresh herbs, if desired, such as chervil or flat-leaf parsley.

1 3/4 pounds scallops

9 ounces fresh pasta, preferably Pasta Nera (see page 181)

2 tablespoons unsalted butter

salt and freshly ground white pepper

2 tablespoons light olive oil

For the saffron sauce:

2 shallots, finely chopped

1 garlic clove

the trim from the scallops, or 2 ounces white fish fillet

1 tablespoon unsalted butter

3/4 cup plus 2 tablespoons medium-dry white wine

a pinch of saffron threads

1 cup whipping cream

salt and freshly ground black pepper

Spiced Ragoût of Shellfish
under a Puff Pastry Lid

THE TECHNIQUE OF BAKING A SOUP UNDER A PUFF PASTRY LID HAS BEEN AROUND FOR A WHILE. THE WHOLE POINT IS THAT IT ADDS INTEREST, AND THEN WHEN YOU BREAK THE PASTRY, YOUR SENSES ARE OVERWHELMED BY THE WONDERFUL AROMAS. **Serves 4**

**9 ounces Puff Pastry
(see pages 182-183)**

1 lobster, about 1 1/2 pounds

12 large shrimp

6 to 7 ounces scallops

**2 egg yolks, lightly beaten,
for glaze**

For soup base:

knob of unsalted butter

2 ounces shallots, chopped

1 ounce fresh ginger root, chopped

1 cup chopped celery

**1 cup chopped celery root
(celeriac)**

2 cups fish stock

1/2 cup whipping cream

1 tablespoon snipped fresh chives

**2 tablespoons chopped
fresh cilantro**

1 teaspoon ground dried chili

On a floured work surface, roll out the puff pastry about 1/8 inch thick. Transfer to a baking sheet and chill for at least 20 minutes.

When it is cold and firm, use an overturned soup bowl in which you will be serving the soup (remember, the bowl must be ovenproof) to estimate the size of the round to cut. It should be 1/4 inch larger in diameter than the bowl to ensure that you will be able to seal the puff securely around the bowl. Cut out the rounds and again place in the refrigerator to chill for 20 minutes.

To make the soup base, in a large saucepan, melt the butter and fry the shallots, ginger, and celery. When they are all soft, add the celery root and the fish stock. Cook over medium heat for about 10 minutes. Add the cream and bring to a boil. Remove from the heat and puree in a blender. Pass through a fine-mesh sieve into a bowl and set aside.

To prepare the seafood, put a large pot of salted water on to boil. First, kill the lobster as directed on page 53, then add to the pot and boil for about 15 minutes. Remove from the pot and refresh in cold water. Then add the shrimp and cook for about 2 minutes. Refresh them in cold water as well. When cool enough to handle, peel off the shells from the shrimp, and remove the meat from the lobster as directed on page 53. Cut the lobster and shrimp into 1/2-inch pieces. Dice the scallops into pieces about the same size.

Preheat the oven to 400 degrees F.

Add the seafood to the pureed soup base along with the herbs and ground chili. Ladle into the soup bowls. Brush the perimeter of the bowls carefully with a little of the egg yolk glaze, then top with the puff rounds and seal the edges. Decorate the top of the puff by brushing with the glaze and then very gently scoring a pattern onto the glaze.

Place the bowls on a sturdy baking sheet and cook in the preheated oven for about 8 minutes. Remember that the bowls will be very hot on removal from the oven and should be lifted out with a thick oven mitt.

Grilled Dublin Bay Prawns
with Garlic Butter

WE ARE BLESSED IN IRELAND WITH PLENTY OF LIVE PRAWNS. BUY YOUR PRAWNS (AND LOBSTERS) ONLY FROM A RELIABLE SOURCE, AS FRESHNESS IS A MOST IMPORTANT FACTOR. SERVE THESE LARGE, DELICIOUS PRAWNS WITH LOTS OF BREAD FOR SOPPING UP THE TASTY GARLIC BUTTER. **Serves 4 as a first course**

To make the butter, boil the white wine with the shallots in a small saucepan until reduced by half. Transfer to a food processor and add the butter, garlic, herbs, and the Pernod, if using. Process until well mixed. Taste the butter carefully for salt and pepper, and add some lemon juice if you feel it needs it.

Preheat the broiler.

Working on a large cutting board with a large chef's knife, split the prawns lengthwise from head to tail. Crack each claw by tapping it with the back of a knife. Arrange the prawns close together on a broiler pan, open side facing upward. Season the prawns lightly with salt and pepper, and spread the garlic butter very generously over the prawns. Slip under the broiler 4 to 6 inches from the heat source. Cook for 5 minutes, or until the prawns are cooked, shaking the pan occasionally to prevent the butter from burning, and to mix in those wonderful juices. Serve immediately. Paul finds the best part of this dish is sucking the shells and claws to savor every last drop of flavor.

12 large, very fresh prawns, preferably with heads on

For the garlic butter:

3/4 cup plus 2 tablespoons dry white wine

2 shallots, finely chopped

1/2 cup plus 1 tablespoon (4 1/2 ounces) unsalted butter, at room temperature

1/2 to 1 tablespoon minced garlic

2 tablespoons chopped fresh parsley

1 tablespoon chopped fresh tarragon

2 tablespoons Pernod (optional)

salt and freshly ground white pepper

squeeze of lemon juice (optional)

CHAPTER SIX

The Ocean

One has only to look at Ireland's geographical location to appreciate what a huge diversity of seafood there is available to her fishing fleets. The pure, cold waters of the Atlantic Ocean lie to her north and west, the Celtic Sea to her south, and the Irish Sea to her east, all rich in fish—and some of the very best in the world at that.

Paul truly believes that he's never seen such quality—so fresh and so continually consistent—anywhere in the world (at such good market prices as well). It's quite strange then that Ireland is not really a fish-eating nation. Perhaps with such an abundance of grass-fed animals, domestic and wild, it didn't seem necessary to go to sea for food. There are some traditional old-fashioned favorites: herring, mackerel, and kipper would be the best known. Lingcod used to be salted and dried and sold inland for winter use. Whiting and plaice (a member of the flounder family) have always been popular with the fish-and-chips shops. Skate (ray), cod, hake, and haddock are all plentiful and moderately priced fish, just waiting to be appreciated more widely. Restaurants need to be encouraged to serve more fish on a regular basis, but not smothered in heavy sauces or overcooked to tasteless dryness as has so often been done in the past. Is it any wonder that customers have tended to be skeptical of fish dishes?

It is quite obvious, when one sees the fantastic quality, that Irish fishermen take great pride in getting their bountiful catch to the markets in pristine condition. They handle the fish with care and respect, icing it properly while on the boats to ensure freshness. One really must appreciate these steps because they do make such a difference in the final product.

Nowadays, with the healthy-diet consciousness becoming more widespread, people are looking for alternatives to their regular fare. More people are trying fish now than ever before, and hopefully learning to appreciate its wholesome goodness as well as its flavor. The first simple step to take is finding a reliable and knowledgeable fishmonger. After you've done that, there's no limit to what your taste buds can learn.

Warm Salad of Fish and Chips

THIS IS A FAVORITE QUICK LUNCH DISH. THE CRISPY FISH AND CHIPS ARE A GREAT CONTRAST TO THE SALAD. IF YOU'RE CAREFUL WITH YOUR PRESENTATION, IT CAN ALSO BE A VERY ELEGANT STARTER. **Serves 4**

1 large baking potato

vegetable oil for deep-frying

salt and freshly ground white pepper

14 ounces monkfish fillets

1 egg, lightly beaten

2 tablespoons whipping cream

3/4 cup all-purpose flour

a few mixed salad leaves

2 tablespoons Vinaigrette Dressing (see page 177)

For the mustard sauce:

2/3 cup whipping cream

2 tablespoons whole-grain mustard

Peel the potato and cut it into wafer-thin slices or matchstick-sized chips. Soak the potato in cold water for about 1 hour to remove excess starch.

Heat the oil in a deep-fat fryer or deep pot to 375 degrees F, or until a cube of bread browns within about 40 seconds. Drain the potato pieces and dry them off with a cloth. Fry in the hot oil for about 4 minutes, or until they are crisp and golden. Transfer to paper towels and season with salt. Keep warm.

Meanwhile, make the mustard sauce: Bring the cream to a boil in a small pan. Simmer for about 1 minute, or until slightly thickened. Remove from the heat and whisk in the mustard.

Slice the monkfish fillets into pieces 1/2 inch thick. Whisk together the egg and the 2 tablespoons cream and rub this vigorously into the monkfish pieces. Dredge the monkfish in the flour, pushing the flour into the fish pieces so that all the cream-egg mixture is absorbed.

Fry the monkfish in the hot oil (again at 375 degrees F) for 3 minutes, or until crisp and nicely brown. Transfer to paper towels and season with salt and pepper.

To serve, toss the salad leaves in the vinaigrette and divide among 4 plates. Top the salad leaves with the fish pieces and the potatoes. Drizzle with the mustard sauce and serve at once.

Skate Meunière
with Creamed Potatoes, Red Wine, and Capers

IN THIS SIMPLE DISH, EACH INGREDIENT DEPENDS ON THE QUALITY OF THE OTHER FOR THE SUCCESS OF THE WHOLE. IF YOU CAN'T GET BEAUTIFUL SKATE, USE ANOTHER FISH SUCH AS HADDOCK. **Serves 6**

To prepare the skate, fillet and skin the skate wings. This can be a difficult job, so perhaps your fishmonger could do it for you. Ask for the bones for your sauce, but the skin can be discarded. Trim the skate fillets into 3-inch squares for easy sautéing.

In a large pan, gently sauté the carrot and onion in 2 tablespoons of the butter until lightly colored. Add the skate bones, garlic, Bouquet Garni, tomato paste, and flour and cook for a further 4 minutes. Add the wine, bring to a boil, and boil until the wine has reduced by two-thirds. Add the stock, return to a boil, reduce the heat, and simmer for 20 minutes.

Strain the sauce through a fine-mesh sieve into a small pan and boil until reduced to a sauce consistency. Season with salt and pepper, then whisk in 1 tablespoon of the butter to mellow the sauce.

To make the creamed potatoes, bring the cream to a boil in a pan, then add it to the potatoes. Stir with a whisk to a very smooth consistency and season with salt and pepper. Set aside in a warm place.

To fry the skate wings, heat the remaining 3 tablespoons butter in a large frying pan over high heat. When the butter is foamy, add the skate and season with salt and pepper. Fry gently for 2 minutes on each side, then add the capers. Remove from the heat and allow to sit in the frying pan while you set up the plates.

To serve, spoon some of the creamed potatoes onto the top ends of warmed plates. Arrange the skate fillets in front of the potatoes, spooning a little of the caper-butter juice from the pan over each piece. Surround with a little of the sauce and garnish with parsley sprigs.

4 1/2 pounds skate (ray) wings

2/3 cup peeled and chopped carrot

1/2 cup chopped onion

6 tablespoons unsalted butter

1 garlic clove, chopped

1 Bouquet Garni (see page 188)

1 tablespoon tomato paste

1 tablespoon all-purpose flour

1 1/2 cups full-bodied red wine

1 cup Brown Chicken Stock (see page 178)

salt and freshly ground black pepper

1/4 cup drained high-quality capers

fresh flat-leaf parsley sprigs

For the creamed potatoes:

7 tablespoons whipping cream

1 recipe Pureed Potatoes (see recipe for Champ, page 139)

salt and freshly ground white pepper

Grilled Dover Sole
with Herb Butter and Grilled Leeks

DOVER SOLE HAS TO BE ONE OF THE LUSHEST FISH AROUND. SERVING IT ON THE BONE LIKE THIS MAY SEEM LAZY, BUT IT ADDS A TREMENDOUS AMOUNT OF FLAVOR AND MOISTURE TO THE DELICATE FLESH. IF YOU PREFER, USE DRY WHITE WINE IN PLACE OF RED WINE. **Serves 4**

4 whole Dover sole, about 1 pound each

salt and freshly ground black pepper

1/2 cup (4 ounces) unsalted butter

4 medium-sized leeks

2 tablespoons light olive oil

For the herb butter:

1 1/2 cups dry red wine

1 shallot, finely chopped

1/2 garlic clove, chopped

1 teaspoon salt

1/2 teaspoon freshly ground black pepper

1/2 teaspoon chopped fresh thyme

1 tablespoon chopped fresh parsley

1 cup plus 2 tablespoons (9 ounces) unsalted butter, finely diced, at room temperature

To make the herb butter, boil the red wine in a small pan with the shallot until the wine has reduced to about 6 tablespoons. Remove from the heat and add the garlic, salt, pepper, and herbs. Add the butter and mash or whisk together the red wine infusion without melting the butter (a food processor does the job in half the time). Transfer to a small bowl and keep at room temperature.

To prepare the Dover sole, cut off the heads at a slight angle and discard. Turn the fish dark skin upward, and with a sharp knife cut across the skin where the tail joins the body. Starting at the cut, use the point of a knife to pry a flap of skin away from the flesh until you can obtain a firm grip on it. Grasp the flap of skin in one hand. With the other, hold down the tail, using a cloth to prevent your fingers from slipping. Firmly and decisively pull the skin up toward the head end, and it will pull right off.

Turn the fish over and grip it by the tail and, using the edge of a knife or a fish scaler, scrape toward the head to remove the scales from the white skin. It is a good idea to scale the fish in a large basin or in a plastic bag to prevent the scales from being scattered around the kitchen. Rinse the fish under cold running water and pat dry on paper towels. This whole process can seem time-consuming, but it is good fun. But if you don't enjoy this type of thing, have your fishmonger ready the fish for you.

Preheat the broiler. Heavily butter a baking sheet.

Season the sole with salt and pepper and lay the fish skin side up on the baking sheet. Smear the skin with the butter and place under the broiler. Allow to cook skin side up for about 7 minutes, basting the fish with the cooking juices every minute or so. Pour off and reserve these cooking juices and add 2 tablespoons of the herb butter to the juices. Cover the fish with aluminum foil and allow to rest away from the heat while you prepare the leeks.

To prepare the leeks, pull away any wilted or old leaves. Cut in half lengthwise and wash under cold running water. Parboil the leeks for 4 minutes in salted boiling water. Refresh the leeks in cold water to set the color, then allow to drain well. Toss the leeks in the olive oil. Place on a baking sheet and broil for about 3 minutes, or until nicely charred and marked.

To serve, carefully lift the fish onto warmed plates and garnish the plates with the grilled leeks. Spoon an equal amount of the herb butter on top of each fish and drizzle each plate with the precious cooking juices from the baking sheet.

Baked Haddock
with Zucchini, Lemon, and Thyme

THIS IS A SIMPLE ONE-PAN DISH THAT CAN BE DONE WITH ANY FISH. **Serves 4**

Preheat the oven to 425 degrees F. Heavily butter a ceramic baking dish with half of the butter.

Lay the zucchini, shallots, and mushrooms in the prepared dish, and season them lightly with salt and pepper. Season the haddock fillets lightly with the salt and pepper, and lay them on top of the vegetables. Use up the rest of the butter by topping each fillet with a generous piece of it. Sprinkle the fish with the lemon juice and thyme.

Cover the dish tightly with aluminum foil. Bake for 8 minutes, or until the fish are opaque throughout. Serve immediately, spooning some of the vegetables and buttery juices onto each plate with the fillets.

4 to 5 tablespoons unsalted butter

2 medium zucchini, sliced or cut into batons

2 shallots, finely chopped

8 firm white mushrooms, sliced

salt and freshly ground white pepper

4 haddock fillets, about 7 ounces each

3 tablespoons fresh lemon juice

1/2 teaspoon fresh thyme leaves or 1/4 teaspoon dried

Salt Chili Turbot
on a Bed of Wilted Greens

INSPIRED BY A CLASSIC CHINESE CULINARY TECHNIQUE, WE HAVE TWISTED THE RECIPE SO THAT THE CHILI APPEARS IN THE SAUCE AND THE SALT TURNS UP AT THE LAST MOMENT AS CRUNCHY SEA SALT SPRINKLED ON TOP. **Serves 4**

For the tomato-chili sauce:

1 1/2 pounds turbot fillets, about 1/2 inch thick

2 ounces baby spinach leaves

2 ounces romaine lettuce leaves

2 ounces arugula

coarse sea salt

2 garlic cloves, finely chopped

7 tablespoons virgin olive oil

8 anchovy fillets, finely crushed

2 fresh chilies

8 plum tomatoes, peeled, seeded, and roughly chopped

juice of 1/2 lemon

salt and freshly ground black pepper

To make the tomato-chili sauce, fry the garlic in a little of the olive oil for 4 minutes over medium-low heat until soft. Add the anchovies, chilies, and tomatoes. Quickly bring to a boil and simmer for 1 minute. Remove from the heat, allow to cool slightly, and then add the remaining olive oil, a little lemon juice, and some salt and pepper to taste. Set aside.

To prepare the turbot, trim the fillets, skinning them if necessary, then divide into 4 equal portions. Set the fillets in a shallow bowl in a Chinese bamboo steamer basket, and season very lightly with salt. Put the basket above boiling water and steam for about 5 minutes, or until opaque throughout. The cooking time will vary greatly according to the thickness of the fillets.

To serve, combine the spinach, lettuce, and arugula, and arrange the greens neatly in the middle of 4 warmed plates. Surround with the tomato-chili sauce. Set the turbot fillets directly on top of the greens so that they will wilt from the heat of the fillets. Finally, sprinkle the turbot fillets with some coarse sea salt.

Steamed Symphony of Seafood
with Saffron Butter Vinaigrette

STEAMING IS A WONDERFULLY FORGIVING TECHNIQUE FOR COOKING COMPLEX DISHES. THIS DISH IS COMPLEX IN THAT YOU HAVE SO MANY SMALL PIECES OF FISH, BUT IT IS SPECTACULAR WHEN IT IS COOKED AND WELL WORTH TRYING. A SELECTION OF ABOUT HALF A DOZEN OR SO VERY FRESH FISH AND SHELLFISH IS NEEDED. USE WHAT IS AVAILABLE TO YOU. THE FOLLOWING ARE JUST EXAMPLES. SERVE WITH BUTTERED SPINACH AND POTATOES. **Serves 4**

Carefully trim the fish fillets, making sure that they are nicely shaped and free of bones. Cut the fillets into appropriate sizes, making sure that you have 4 pieces of each fish being used. Save the trimmings and bones for infusing the sauce.

To make the butter vinaigrette, clarify the butter by bringing it to a simmer in a small pan. Skim off any froth that comes to the surface. When the surface has cleared, let the butter settle and simply pour the butter off, leaving behind any watery, milky liquid. Discard the milky liquid and reserve the butter.

In a small pan, bring the wine to a simmer with the shallot, saffron threads, and fish trimmings and simmer until the liquid has reduced to about 3 tablespoons. Add the fish stock and simmer again until you have 7 to 7 1/2 ounces remaining. Strain this liquid through a fine sieve. Season with salt and pepper. Add the tomatoes, tarragon, and clarified butter and the vinaigrette is ready.

To steam the fish, butter a large steaming basket and arrange the pieces of fish and shellfish carefully in it. Season with salt only (pepper at this stage makes the fish look dirty). Place over a pan of boiling water, cover, and steam for about 4 minutes, or until the fish is opaque throughout.

To serve, arrange some spinach as a bed for the fish and shellfish. Arrange the pieces attractively on top of the spinach, and spoon the butter vinaigrette over the top.

about 4 to 5 ounces each of 6 to 8 fish or shellfish such salmon, lemon sole, hake, monkfish, haddock, prawns, mussels, and scallops

For the butter vinaigrette:

1/2 cup plus 2 tablespoons (5 ounces) unsalted butter

2/3 cup dry white wine

1 shallot, finely chopped

pinch of saffron threads

2/3 cup fish stock

salt and freshly ground white pepper

2 tomatoes, peeled, seeded, and chopped

2 fresh tarragon sprigs, chopped

Chargrilled Squid
with Noodles, Chili, and Cilantro

SQUID CAN BE AN ACQUIRED TASTE, BUT WE'VE FOUND THAT OUR CUSTOMERS FIND IT MORE APPROACHABLE COOKED THIS WAY. **Serves 4**

1 pound squid

vegetable oil

salt and freshly ground white pepper

5 ounces cellophane noodles

Asian sesame oil

For the vinaigrette:

1 ounce fresh ginger root

4 tablespoons rice wine vinegar

1 tablespoon mushroom soy or dark soy sauce

2 tablespoons Asian chili sauce

1 bunch fresh cilantro, picked and roughly chopped

salt and freshly ground white pepper

3/4 cup vegetable oil

1/2 cup Asian sesame oil

For the pepper garnish:

3/4 cup rice wine vinegar

3 tablespoons sugar

1 red bell pepper

To garnish:

a few mixed salad greens

sesame seeds, toasted

chopped fresh cilantro

Prepare a charcoal fire.

To make the vinaigrette, combine all the ingredients except the oils in a bowl and whisk until the salt has dissolved. Slowly whisk in the oils. Adjust the seasoning to taste.

To make the pepper garnish, bring the rice wine vinegar and sugar to a boil in a small pan. Cut the pepper into quarters lengthwise and remove the seeds. Cut into thin slices and add to the vinegar mixture, or "gastric." Simmer for 10 minutes. Set aside in the liquid.

To prepare each squid, separate the head and tentacles from the body and discard the stiff cartilage quill. Cut the head off just above the eyes and reserve the tentacles. Remove the purplish skin and rinse the meat thoroughly in cold water. Cut the body into 1 1/2-inch pieces. Coat the squid pieces in a little vegetable oil and season with salt and pepper. Set aside.

Soak the cellophane noodles for about 15 minutes in warm water and drain. Some cellophane noodles require no cooking if they have been soaked, but depending on the type you have, you may need to cook them for 1 to 2 minutes in a pot of salted boiling water. Either way, drain and toss with a little sesame oil. Place a pile in the middle of the plate. Drain the pepper slices and arrange them and the salad leaves attractively around the noodles (the noodles are served at room temperature).

Quickly grill the squid for about 45 seconds over a very hot charcoal fire (or in a cast-iron pan or stove-top grill). Serve immediately with the vinaigrette sprinkled liberally on top. Garnish with the sesame seeds and lots of fresh cilantro.

CHAPTER SEVEN

The Duck Pond

There have probably always been ducks in Ireland. Farmyards would have had their few along with the chickens, and shooting, a popular sport in the countryside, would have yielded wild ones. Even though it is such a commonly found bird, duck is nevertheless often avoided by many. Surely this must just be out of lack of knowledge or confidence in what to do with it. That is a great shame because it tends to have more flavor than chicken without coming across as too gamy or strong.

Perhaps it is the composition of the duck that seems off-putting. Ducks have a large frame, comparatively little meat, and a much higher fat content than chicken. However, these qualities do have their benefits. Duck carcasses, so full of robust and hearty flavor, are fantastic for stocks and soups. The fat can also be used to the cook's advantage. Most importantly, it helps keep the meat moist during cooking. It can be trimmed off, rendered (boiled down), and used as a cooking medium for other products.

Don't think ducks should be saved for holiday meals only. They are relatively inexpensive nowadays and widely available. The simplest (and one of the tastiest) ways to cook a duck is just to roast it whole. Simply season it with some salt and pepper and put it in a medium-hot oven (350 degrees F) for about 2 hours. Duck is one of the most popular dishes in our restaurant, which leads us to believe that people really do appreciate it.

Don't forget the possibility of goose, either. Because of its size, it is usually reserved for the bigger family occasions, but most recipes for duck can be applied to goose as well.

The first three recipes in this chapter have been designed to create an elaborate meal using just one duck. You can use the carcass, the giblets, the wings, and the duck fillets for the soup; the legs and the fat for the crispy duck *confit;* and the breast meat for the peppered duck breast.

Duck Soup
with Cilantro Dumplings

CONSOMMÉ CAN SOMETIMES BE A BIT LIGHT FOR THOSE WITH A HEARTY APPETITE. THE ADDITION OF DUMPLINGS OR NOODLES CAN BE THE PERFECT SOLUTION AND IT ALSO ADDS ANOTHER DIMENSION. **Serves 4**

To make the stock, put the carcass in a large pot with just enough water to cover. Bring to a boil, skimming away any fat and scum that come to the surface. Add the onion, carrot, garlic, Bouquet Garni, and cloves, cover partially, and simmer gently for about 2 hours. Strain through a fine-mesh sieve into a clean saucepan.

To make the dumplings, mince the liver, heart, gizzard, inner fillets, and the bacon. Add the onion, bread, garlic, egg, flour, salt and pepper to taste, and cilantro and mix together until just combined. Form into walnut-sized balls. Bring a large saucepan of salted water to a boil, add the dumplings, and poach for about 5 minutes, or until cooked through. Using a slotted spoon, scoop the dumplings from the water.

To serve, bring the stock to serving temperature and add the dumplings. Check for seasoning. Divide the lettuce and tomato among the bowls and then ladle the stock and dumplings over the top.

For the stock:

1 duck carcass, neck, and wings

1 cup chopped onion

1 cup peeled and chopped carrot

1/2 garlic bulb

1 Bouquet Garni (see page 188)

3 whole cloves

For the dumplings:

1 each duck liver, heart, and gizzard

2 inner fillets duck breast

2 slices fatty bacon

1 small onion, finely chopped

2 slices bread, crusts removed, soaked in milk, and squeezed dry

1 garlic clove, minced

1 egg, lightly beaten

1/3 cup all-purpose flour

salt and freshly ground white pepper

2 tablespoons chopped fresh cilantro

2 lettuce leaves, finely shredded

1 tomato, diced

OVERLEAF:
Left: Crispy Duck Confit with Chinese Spices (page 76)

Right: Roast Spiced Duck Breast with Honey and Soy Sauce (page 78)

Crispy Duck Confit
with Chinese Spices

THE BEST WAY TO DESCRIBE THE TEXTURE OF A CONFIT IS TO COMPARE IT TO THAT CHINESE FAVORITE, CRISPY AROMATIC DUCK. IT SIMPLY FALLS OFF THE BONE, MOIST SHREDS INFUSED WITH THE FLAVOR OF THE MARINADE. **Serves 2**

2 duck legs

2 tablespoons chopped fresh ginger root

1 garlic clove, chopped

1 teaspoon white peppercorns

1/2 teaspoon ground anise

4 tablespoons coarse sea salt

fat from the duck carcass

2/3 cup water

peanut oil or rendered chicken fat

For the sauce:

1 tablespoon rendered duck fat

1 shallot, chopped

1 teaspoon chopped fresh ginger root

2/3 cup duck stock or water

2 whole star anise

1 teaspoon honey

1 teaspoon hoisin sauce

a pinch of red pepper flakes

soy sauce

salt

To garnish:

1/2 cucumber

1 scallion, finely chopped

Twenty-four hours before using, marinate the duck legs: Place them in a dish and scatter the ginger, white peppercorns, ground anise, and sea salt evenly over the legs. Chop the duck fat roughly and place in a pan. Add the water and simmer for about 2 hours, or until the fat begins to look clear. Strain the fat into a clean pan ready to cook the duck legs.

Rinse the excess spices off the marinated legs, removing the salt as well. Put the legs into the duck fat (if the fat does not completely cover the legs, top it up with the peanut oil or chicken fat). Simmer the legs very gently for 1 1/2 hours, or until they are very tender. Allow to cool in the fat.

To make the sauce, in a pan heat the duck fat and fry the shallot and ginger gently until lightly browned. Add the stock, star anise, honey, hoisin sauce, and red pepper flakes. Simmer until the mixture has reached a sauce consistency that will coat the back of a spoon. Correct the seasoning with soy sauce and, if needed, salt.

Peel the cucumber. Make nice long ribbons by peeling very heavily with a vegetable peeler.

Preheat the broiler or the oven to 400 degrees F.

To serve, crisp up the duck legs by placing them skin side up underneath the hot broiler or in the preheated oven for 5 minutes. Arrange the cucumber ribbons on warmed plates. Set the legs on top, scatter the scallion over the legs, and surround with a little sauce.

Peppered Duck Breast
with Spinach, Mushrooms, and Cream

PEKING OR AYLESBURY DUCK BREASTS, WITHOUT THE SKIN, ARE PERFECT FOR FLASH-FRYING. THEY CAN BE COOKED AS SIMPLY AS ANY STEAK AND LEND THEMSELVES TO ALMOST ANY RECIPE. HERE WE COULDN'T RESIST GIVING THE BREASTS THE CLASSIC PEPPER STEAK TREATMENT. **Serves 2**

Spread the cracked peppercorns on the duck breasts, pressing down on the pepper to encrust the breasts. Season the breasts with salt. Heat the butter and oil in a frying pan and fry the duck breasts gently for 3 minutes on each side for medium-rare, or 5 minutes on each side for well done. Remove the duck breasts from the pan and keep warm.

Deglaze the pan with the Cognac and duck stock, stirring well to scrape up the meat juices. Add the cream and simmer to reduce to the sauce consistency preferred. Keep warm.

To prepare the garnish, season the spinach leaves with salt and fry in 1 tablespoon of the butter until wilted. Fry the mushrooms in the remaining 1 tablespoon butter with the oil until tender. Mix the two together.

To serve, spoon the spinach and mushroom mixture onto warmed plates. Slice the duck breasts and arrange on top of the spinach. Surround with the warm sauce.

2 tablespoons black peppercorns, cracked

2 duck breasts, skin removed

salt

3 tablespoons unsalted butter

2 tablespoons vegetable oil

4 tablespoons Cognac

7 tablespoons reduced duck stock

7 tablespoons whipping cream

To garnish:

4 ounces spinach leaves

salt

2 tablespoons unsalted butter

4 ounces fresh button mushrooms

1 tablespoon vegetable oil

Roast Spiced Duck Breast
with Honey and Soy Sauce

THIS RECIPE GIVES YOU THE CLASSIC RESTAURANT TECHNIQUE FOR COOKING BARBARY DUCK BREASTS. ONCE PRACTICED, YOU'LL FIND IT SIMPLE AND FOOLPROOF. **Serves 4**

2 large, boneless Barbary duck breasts, about 12 ounces each

salt and freshly ground white pepper

cayenne pepper

1 tablespoon chopped fresh ginger root

a pinch of red pepper flakes

2 tablespoons honey

2 tablespoons mushroom soy sauce

1 tablespoon tomato ketchup

2 tablespoons medium-dry sherry

1/2 cup chicken stock

fresh lime juice or soy sauce

Preheat the oven to 425 degrees F.

To prepare and cook the duck breasts, trim them and lightly score the skin side with a sharp knife. Season the skin with salt, turn the breasts over, and season with salt, white pepper, and a little cayenne pepper.

Heat a dry ovenproof frying pan over medium heat. Place the duck breasts skin side down in the hot pan and let cook for about 5 minutes, or until the skin is nicely golden and crisp. Pour off any excess fat, turn the breasts over, and cook for about 1 minute to seal the other side. Turn them back onto their skin sides and place the pan in the preheated oven for about 4 minutes for medium-rare, 6 minutes for medium, or 10 minutes for well done. Remove the duck breasts from the pan and let them rest while you make the sauce.

To make the sauce, pour off any fat left in the pan. Add the ginger, red pepper flakes, honey, mushroom soy, ketchup, sherry, and chicken stock. Boil for 2 minutes to thicken to a sauce consistency that will coat the back of a spoon. Taste the sauce carefully and add a squeeze of lime juice or bit of soy sauce if you feel that it needs it.

To serve, slice the duck breasts thinly and arrange on warmed plates. Pour over a little sauce and serve at once.

Warm Salad of Sautéed Duck Livers
with Sliced Potatoes and Green Beans

SOAKING THE LIVERS IN MILK TAKES AWAY ANY UNPLEASANT, BITTER TASTES. KEEP THEM PINK IN THE MIDDLE SO THEY RETAIN THEIR SILKY TEXTURE. **Serves 4**

To prepare the livers, trim off any sinew and dark spots. In a bowl, soak the livers in the milk for at least 2 hours, or overnight if possible.

To make the hazelnut vinaigrette, whisk together the mustard, wine vinegar, salt, and white pepper in a small bowl until the salt has dissolved. Slowly whisk in the oils, whisking constantly. Taste and adjust the seasoning.

To prepare the vegetables, cook the potatoes in their skins in salted boiling water until tender, then drain and refresh in cold water. Peel off the skin and slice into rounds. Season with salt and pepper. Drizzle with a little of the vinaigrette and keep in a warm place.

Cook the green beans in salted water for about 5 minutes, or until tender, then drain and refresh in plenty of cold water. Drain and cut into 1/2-inch lengths. Season with salt and pepper. Add the shallot, hazelnuts, and a few tablespoons of the hazelnut vinaigrette. Don't add the vinaigrette too early or the beans will lose their bright green color. (Reserve any remaining vinaigrette for another use.)

To sauté the livers, take the livers out of the milk and drain them on paper towels. Season generously with salt and pepper. Heat the butter in a large frying pan over high heat until it foams. Add the livers in a single layer and allow them to brown, without shaking them, for about 3 minutes. Turn them over and cook for a further 1 minute. The livers should remain slightly pink inside.

To serve, spoon the sliced potatoes onto the center of warmed plates and surround with the green bean mixture. Arrange the livers on top of the potatoes and serve at once.

1 pound duck livers

1 cup milk

5 ounces baby new potatoes

salt and freshly ground white pepper

4 ounces slender green beans

1 shallot, finely chopped

1 tablespoon hazelnuts, toasted and chopped

4 tablespoons unsalted butter

For the hazelnut vinaigrette:

1 teaspoon Dijon mustard

2 tablespoons white wine vinegar

salt and freshly ground white pepper

1/2 cup hazelnut oil

4 tablespoons peanut or sunflower oil

Marsala Crème Brûlée

DUCK YOLKS DEFINITELY GIVE A CREAMIER RESULT TO THIS SIMPLE DESSERT. THE SLIGHTLY LOWER RATIO OF EGGS TO MILK AND CREAM ALSO HELPS PREVENT THAT "EGGINESS" ALL TOO OFTEN FOUND IN CUSTARDS. JEANNE DOESN'T USUALLY ENJOY CUSTARDS, YET SHE FINDS THIS ONE ABSOLUTELY LUSH. IT IS DELICIOUS SERVED WITH A COOKIE ON THE SIDE. A SHORTBREAD OF SOME SORT IS OUR FAVORITE (SEE PAGE 186).

Serves 4 to 6

3/4 cup milk

3/4 cup whipping or light cream

1/4 vanilla bean, split lengthwise

1/2 cup plus 1 tablespoon superfine sugar

3 tablespoons water

5 duck egg yolks

1 whole duck egg

2 tablespoons Marsala (optional)

1/4 cup granulated sugar

Preheat the oven to 300 degrees F. Put the milk, cream, and vanilla bean in a pan and bring to a boil. Set aside to let the vanilla infuse.

Place half of the superfine sugar in a small heavy-bottomed saucepan with the water. Boil until the mixture turns a light caramel color, occasionally brushing down the sides of the pan with a pastry brush dipped in water to ensure the mixture doesn't crystallize. Remove from the heat and carefully pour the caramel into the milk mixture. Place the milk-caramel mixture over low heat for a couple of minutes, just to let the caramel dissolve.

Whisk the egg yolks, whole egg, and remaining superfine sugar together until light and pale and the sugar has dissolved. Whisking this mixture continuously, slowly pour in the milk mixture and whisk until thoroughly blended. Add the Marsala, if using, then strain through a conical sieve or other fine-mesh sieve.

Pour the mixture into ovenproof serving bowls, dividing it evenly, and place them in a roasting pan. Add hot water to the roasting pan to reach halfway up the sides of the bowls. Cover the pan completely with plastic wrap to prevent a crust from forming on the custards while cooking. Place in the preheated oven and cook for about 30 minutes, or until set. The mixture should still wobble slightly if you shake the bowl.

Remove from the oven, remove the plastic wrap, and leave to cool in the roasting pan of water. Chill the custards in the refrigerator.

Preheat a broiler. Sprinkle a thin, even layer of granulated sugar over the top of the chilled custards and place the bowls on a baking sheet. Slip under the broiler until evenly caramelized. (Alternatively, a blow-torch can be used for this step.) The sugar will melt, then harden to a crisp, golden caramel in just a minute or so. Serve at once.

CHAPTER EIGHT

The Game Larder

Game—such a simple word and yet think of the romantic images it conjures up. Grand hunts on stately great estates, aristocratic gentry dressed in splendid style, crisp, chilly mornings, vibrant autumn colors, a great tradition from another era. But game is no longer the privilege of the upper classes. In fact, it is widely available here in Ireland since there is so much being farmed. One can actually enjoy venison, rabbit, quail, partridge, and pheasant without being at all involved in sport.

Nearly all the various types of farms raise their stocks sympathetically. That is, the animals or birds feed on natural foods and live in natural or near natural surroundings, therefore producing a totally organic product as a result. This is great for the public image, especially when one hears all the scary reports of the drugs and chemicals that are so widespread in other livestock rearing. Most game is remarkably lean; venison, in fact, has less fat and cholesterol than any other red meat, making it a viable alternative for a healthful diet.

All game does need to be hung, usually anywhere from several days to just over a week. This does two important things: It tenderizes the meat and it also develops the flavor, although, of course, there are endless debates about the merits of shorter or longer hanging times and so on. Older, tougher animals will also benefit from being marinated before cooking, as this helps to tenderize the meat.

Because of its leanness, game is almost always wrapped or larded with fat to ensure that it doesn't have a chance to dry out during the cooking process. It is not always necessary though. A careful eye, frequent bastings, and shorter cooking times can also overcome the dryness.

Game of delicate flavor, quail or partridge for example, do best when prepared simply. Plainly roasted or grilled, the fine qualities can speak for themselves. Traditionally, large game is matched with rich ingredients. The robust flavors can carry wine, spirits, cream, and spices. Often the richness of the meat is offset by the light tartness of a fruit: orange or kumquat sauce, red currant or cranberry jelly, compote of plums, cherries, apricots, or grapes, to suggest but a few. Many game recipes are interchangeable as long as you bear in mind that the length of cooking times would need to be adjusted.

Most butchers and many supermarkets are now reliable sources of game. Venison distributed by the Irish Deer Farmers' Association is quality controlled. Rabbits can frequently be seen sitting beside chickens on the shelf, as can quail, pheasants, and other game. The wonderful thing is they are remarkably reasonable in price. It's time the old image of game as expensive and exclusive went out the window.

Loin of Hare
with Bacon and Irish Whiskey Cream

HARE, A LARGE RELATIVE OF THE RABBIT, IS A FOOD THAT MOST PEOPLE JUST DON'T LIKE. YET TO US, IT'S ONE OF THE TASTIEST AND BEST VALUE ITEMS AROUND. INTRODUCE YOURSELF TO IT BY TRYING IT AT YOUR MOST TRUSTED RESTAURANT, OR JUST TRY THIS RECIPE. BUSHMILL'S IS THE BEST WHISKEY TO USE. SERVE WITH SOMETHING LIKE THE ROASTED VEGETABLES ON PAGE 88. **Serves 6**

To make the spice mixture, grind all the spices together in a small mortar with a pestle or in a spice grinder.

Slice the hare loin into 12 even-sized medallions and sprinkle the meat evenly with the spice mixture. Drizzle 2 tablespoons of the whiskey over them. Wrap each medallion with a slice of bacon around its circumference and fix it in place with a wooden toothpick.

In a heavy frying pan, heat the oil over high heat and add the butter. When the butter foams, fry the medallions for about 3 minutes on each side. Pour the remaining 3 tablespoons whiskey into the pan and ignite it to flame the hare. Remove the meat and allow it to rest in a warm place while finishing the sauce. Add the cream and the stock to the pan and boil over high heat until a sauce consistency is achieved.

Place 2 medallions on each warmed individual plate and pour the sauce around the medallions.

1 1/4 pounds boneless hare loin, well trimmed

2 slices bacon

5 tablespoons Irish whiskey

1 tablespoon vegetable oil

1 tablespoon unsalted butter

1 cup Brown Chicken Stock (see page 178)

1/2 cup whipping cream

For the spice mixture:

6 juniper berries

2 whole cloves

1/4 teaspoon dried thyme

1/2 teaspoon whole black peppercorns

1/2 teaspoon salt

Stuffed Quail
with Buttered Risotto

WE FIND THAT QUAIL IS THE MOST APPROACHABLE OF ALL GAME BIRDS. IT'S FORGIVING TO COOK AND IT
LENDS ITSELF TO ALL SORTS OF RECIPES. ASK YOUR BUTCHER TO BONE THE QUAIL. **Serves 4**

8 boneless quail

For the risotto:

7 tablespoons unsalted butter

1 small onion, finely chopped

2/3 cup Arborio rice

3 cups chicken stock, heated

**salt and freshly ground
black pepper**

For the stuffing:

5 to 6 ounces spinach

1 shallot, chopped

1 garlic clove, chopped

1 to 2 slices bacon, diced

**1/2 ounce dried porcini
mushrooms, soaked for 15
minutes in hot water, drained,
and diced**

5 tablespoons unsalted butter

**4 to 5 ounces chicken livers,
trimmed**

1 tablespoon pine nuts, toasted

**salt and freshly ground
black pepper**

To garnish:

**a few fresh rosemary or thyme
sprigs (optional)**

Preheat the oven to 400 degrees F. Butter a roasting pan.

To make the risotto, melt one-third of the butter in a heavy-bottomed
saucepan and fry the onion over medium heat until soft and translucent.
Add the rice and stir to coat with the butter for 1 to 2 minutes. Then add
a ladleful of the chicken stock and cook, stirring frequently, until absorbed.
Continue adding the stock a ladleful at a time, allowing each addition to
be absorbed before adding more. After about 20 minutes, all of the stock
will have been added and the rice will be tender but still firm to the bite.
Season to taste. Set aside in a warm place.

Meanwhile, make the stuffing: Blanch the spinach with a little water over
a high heat for 1 to 2 minutes until wilted, then drain and squeeze out
any excess water. In a large frying pan, fry the shallot, garlic, bacon, and
porcini in the butter over medium heat until soft. Add the chicken livers
and pine nuts and cook for a few minutes until they are just browned.
Chop this mixture roughly. Add the spinach and mix together thoroughly.
Season with salt and pepper.

Stuff each quail with one-eighth of the mixture, sealing the birds closed
by pulling the skin over the opening. Place in the buttered roasting pan.

Roast in the preheated oven for 10 to 15 minutes. Because the bird is so
small and the filling is already cooked and warm, it should not take any
longer.

To serve, stir the remaining butter into the warm risotto and place 1 to 2
spoonfuls in the center of each of the warmed plates to make a bed for
the quail. Place 2 birds on each plate and garnish with herb sprigs, if
desired. Serve immediately.

Roast Partridge
with Bacon, Garlic, and Thyme

THIS IS A GREAT RECIPE FOR MOST GAME BIRDS. TRY IT WITH PIGEON, PHEASANT, OR GROUSE. **Serves 2**

Preheat the oven to 425 degrees F.

Season the birds inside and out with salt and pepper and stuff 5 garlic cloves and a sprig of fresh thyme inside each bird. Drape the bacon slices over each bird and truss into place with kitchen string.

Heat the oil and 1 tablespoon of the butter in a large ovenproof pan until the butter is foaming and very hot. Add the partridges and fry briefly on all sides. Turn the birds onto their sides, place in the preheated oven, and roast for 8 to 10 minutes on each side. Remove from the oven, turn the birds breast down, and allow the birds to rest for 5 minutes. Remove from the pan.

Using the same pan that the partridges were cooked in, sauté the shallots in a little of the butter. Meanwhile, untie the birds and remove the bacon, thyme sprigs, and the garlic cloves. Discard the sprigs. Chop the bacon into 1/4-inch pieces. Set aside with the garlic cloves.

Cut off the legs and the breasts from the birds and keep in a warm place. Chop the carcass and livers and add to the shallots. Cook gently for a few minutes. Add the stock, 1 of the remaining thyme sprigs, and 2 of the garlic cloves. Simmer for 5 minutes, then strain through a fine-mesh sieve into a small pan. Boil until reduced to a sauce consistency that coats the back of a spoon. Whisk in a tablespoon of butter and season with salt and pepper. Strip a few leaves from the remaining thyme sprig and add to the sauce.

To serve, fry the reserved bacon pieces and the remaining garlic cloves gently in the remaining butter until the bacon starts to crisp up and the garlic begins to brown. Make sure the partridges are still warm and then arrange on warmed serving plates. Pour over a little sauce and garnish with the fried garlic and bacon pieces.

2 young partridges, cleaned, livers reserved

salt and freshly ground black pepper

10 garlic cloves, blanched for 10 minutes

4 fresh thyme sprigs

6 slices bacon

2 tablespoons light olive oil

1/2 cup (4 ounces) unsalted butter

2 shallots, sliced

1 cup Brown Chicken Stock (see page 178)

OVERLEAF:
Left: Roast Partridge with Bacon, Garlic, and Thyme
Right: Warm Game Tart with Roasted Winter Vegetables and Green Peppercorns (page 88)

Warm Game Tart
with Roasted Winter Vegetables and Green Peppercorns

WE'VE ALWAYS LOVED A GAME TART. IN FACT, WE COULD TACKLE ONE NEARLY ANY WINTERY EVENING. USE A SELECTION OF SUITABLE GAME AND A GOOD-QUALITY SAUSAGE MEAT FROM YOUR BUTCHER. YOU CAN CHOOSE WHICHEVER VEGETABLES YOU LIKE OR HAVE ON HAND. PUFF PASTRY IS AVAILABLE IN MOST DELICATESSENS AND SUPERMARKETS, BUT IF YOU CAN MAKE YOUR OWN, ALL THE BETTER. **Serves 6**

For the filling:

12 ounces game meat such as pheasant legs, venison shoulder, hare, and pigeon, well trimmed

5 ounces pork sausage meat

3 ounces bacon

3 ounces back fat

1 tablespoon brandy

1 shallot, chopped

1 garlic clove, chopped

1 tablespoon chopped fresh parsley

1 tablespoon chopped fresh thyme or 1/2 teaspoon dried

1 teaspoon freshly ground black pepper

1/2 teaspoon salt

7 ounces Puff Pastry, home-made (see pages 182-183) or store-bought

1 egg yolk, lightly beaten

For the sauce:

2/3 cup whipping cream

2/3 cup meat gravy or stock

2 tablespoons whiskey or Cognac

1 tablespoon whole green peppercorns, lightly crushed

salt

To make the filling, check that all the game is well trimmed, that it has no "off" bits or tough sinews. Slice all the meat and fat into manageable pieces about 1 by 3 inches. Combine all the filling ingredients together in a bowl and mix them roughly. Put the mixture through the coarse blade of your mincer or chop very finely by hand. Beat well with a wooden spoon or mix with your hands to ensure that it is blended thoroughly. Form into a ball, wrap in plastic wrap, and refrigerate.

On a floured surface, roll out the puff pastry into two 12-inch squares no thicker than 1/8 inch. Chill these 2 sheets for at least 20 minutes.

When they are cold, bring out one piece and cut it into a large circle about 9 1/2 inches in diameter. The easiest way to accomplish this is to use an overturned bowl or plate as a guide. Brush this base completely with the egg yolk, taking care not to let it drip over the sides.

Place the filling in the center of the base and with your hands, pat into an even dome shape. There should be a perimeter of at least 1 1/2 to 2 1/2 inches of puff pastry all the way around the filling.

Take the other piece of puff pastry from the refrigerator and quickly reapply egg wash to the perimeter of the base before laying the second piece on top. Carefully, with your hands, gently pat this piece in place, shaping the puff pastry over the filling and sealing the edges together. Try not to let there be any big air pockets inside, and try not to stretch the top sheet or it will lose shape during cooking.

Brush the whole top of the tart with the egg yolk, making sure not to let it drip over the edges, and cut the two edges so that they are even with each other. Pierce a small hole in the center of the top to let the steam be released during cooking, and decorate with the egg yolk wash as you like. You can achieve this by using the back of a knife, the tines of a fork, or even a wooden toothpick. Return to the refrigerator again to chill for 20 minutes. Meanwhile, preheat the oven to 350 degrees F.

Bake the tart in the preheated oven for about 30 minutes, or until golden brown.

To make the sauce, combine the cream and meat gravy or stock in a small pan and boil until thickened to a sauce consistency. Add the whiskey or Cognac and the green peppercorns (lightly crushing them helps to release their flavor and aroma). Simmer again over low heat for 1 to 2 minutes, and then check for seasoning. Add salt as needed. Keep warm.

To prepare the vegetables, boil or steam them until they are just cooked. Allow them to cool slightly. Heat the butter in a large pan until it is foamy and is just turning brown. Throw all the vegetables in at once and allow them to cook gently in the butter for about 5 minutes. Turn them gently from time to time to ensure that they are all coated with the butter. Season with salt and pepper.

To serve, present the tart at the table as a whole, with the vegetables either surrounding it on the plate or on the side in their own serving bowl. Cut the tart into individual portions, serve the vegetables, and pass the sauce so that each may take as much or as little as preferred.

For the vegetables:

2 pounds prepared mixed vegetables such as carrots, potatoes, Brussels sprouts, mushrooms, and baby onions

1/2 cup (4 ounces) plus 1 tablespoon unsalted butter

salt and freshly ground black pepper

Peppered Leg of Venison
with Hot-and-Sour Cabbage

A WELL-HUNG HAUNCH OF YOUNG VENISON IS AT LEAST AS NICE TO EAT AS THE LOIN OR FILLET. THE TECHNIQUE HERE FOR SEPARATING THE LEG MUSCLES MEANS THAT YOU'RE LEFT WITH SINEW-FREE "LOIN" FROM THE LEG. **Serves 6**

1 haunch of venison, about 5 1/2 pounds

cracked black peppercorns

salt

2 tablespoons unsalted butter

1 tablespoon vegetable oil

For the hot-and-sour cabbage:

2 tablespoons unsalted butter

1 head red cabbage, finely sliced

4 tablespoons sherry vinegar

2 eating apples, peeled, cored, and chopped

2 tablespoons raisins

1 tablespoon chopped fresh ginger root

2 tablespoons sugar

1/2 teaspoon freshly ground white pepper

salt

For the sauce:

4 tablespoons sherry vinegar

4 tablespoons meat stock or gravy (optional)

1 1/4 cups whipping cream

salt and freshly ground black pepper

Preheat the oven to 375 degrees F. To cook the cabbage, melt the butter in a large, heavy-bottomed pan. Add the cabbage, sherry vinegar, and salt. Cover and cook over low heat for about 1 hour.

Stir in the apples, raisins, ginger, and sugar and cook gently for another 30 minutes. Finally, add the white pepper and check the seasoning to see if it needs more sugar or salt.

Meanwhile, cook the venison and sauce: Trim the outside of the haunch to remove any sinew and fat. Work carefully to see that you don't remove too much. Separate each large muscle one at a time and place them to one side. Reserve the trim, shin, and very small muscles for another use. Roll the large muscles in cracked black pepper and season them with salt.

Heat a large ovenproof frying pan with the butter and oil and fry the pieces of venison until they have a nice color on all sides. Place them in the preheated oven for 5 minutes for medium-rare or 8 minutes for medium to well done.

Remove the venison pieces from the pan and allow them to rest in a warm place. To make the sauce, pour off any fat from the pan and add the sherry vinegar. Place on the stove top. Scrape the bottom of the pan with a wooden spoon to loosen all the delicious, caramelized juices. Reduce the sherry vinegar over medium-high heat to 1 tablespoon, then add the stock or gravy, if using, and the cream. Reduce by boiling quickly to form a sauce consistency. Season with salt and pepper.

To serve, spoon some piping-hot cabbage onto warmed plates. Slice the venison pieces and arrange the slices neatly on top of the cabbage. Pour over a little sauce and it's ready to serve.

Emincé of Pheasant
with a Wild Mushroom Cream

THE BIGGEST PROBLEM WITH PHEASANT IS ITS TENDENCY TO DRY OUT DURING COOKING. THIS SIMPLE RECIPE GIVES YOU LOTS OF CONTROL TO PREVENT THIS FROM HAPPENING. CHICKEN, GUINEA FOWL, OR RABBIT CAN BE USED IN PLACE OF THE PHEASANT. **Serves 4**

Soak the dried morels in warm water to cover for 30 minutes. Remove them and check that they are free of dirt. Slice the larger ones in half and leave the small ones whole.

Remove the inside fillet from each pheasant breast. Push the breast firmly onto a cutting board and slice at an acute angle into 4 scallops. You now have 5 pieces including the fillet, which makes 1 portion. Repeat this process with the other 3 breasts.

Heat 4 tablespoons of the butter in a large sauté pan until it starts to foam. Add the pheasant pieces in a single layer. Cook gently for 45 seconds on each side, then transfer all the pieces from the pan to a plate.

In the same pan, melt the remaining 1 tablespoon butter and fry the shallots until soft and translucent. Add the white wine, Madeira, and morels and cook gently until most of the liquid has evaporated. Add the cream and the chicken stock, if using (for a lighter sauce), and season with salt and pepper. Simmer gently for about 5 minutes until a sauce consistency has formed.

Meanwhile, prepare the cabbage: Immerse the cabbage leaves in a pan of salted boiling water for a minute or so until wilted, drain very well, and transfer to a large frying with plenty of butter. Sauté until tender, then season with salt and pepper. Arrange a little of the cabbage on each warmed individual plate.

Bring the sauce to a boil, then add the pheasant pieces. Let the sauce slowly return to a simmer, then spoon 5 pheasant pieces and plenty of the sauce onto each plate. Serve at once.

1 ounce dried morel mushrooms

4 pheasant breasts, skinned and boned

5 tablespoons unsalted butter

salt and freshly ground black pepper

2 shallots, finely chopped

7 tablespoons dry white wine

4 tablespoons Madeira

1 cup whipping cream

7 tablespoons chicken stock (optional)

salt and freshly ground white pepper

For the sautéed cabbage:

Savoy cabbage leaves

unsalted butter for sautéing

salt and freshly ground black pepper

CHAPTER NINE

The Pastures

Ireland seems like the perfect place to raise cows and sheep. Its superb pastures are lush and green, and the pure air, abundant rainfall, and fresh winds keep them just so. It is a stress-free, disease-free environment, unpolluted and unravaged by modern industry. It is these factors that contribute to Ireland's producing some of the finest beef and lamb, exported all over Europe and to places farther afield.

There was always some pork available in Ireland, as every farmyard had pigs and at least one was usually slaughtered each year, and it used to be that cattle were just kept for milk and milk products. It was only when an animal was old and rendered useless that it would be butchered. However, even then it was realized that beef was rich and generous in flavor, and when the great estates of the English started to keep huge herds of cattle, beef gained in popularity and quickly became established as the traditional highlight of festive days.

Various forms of preservation had to be developed, for only a certain amount could be used fresh. As a result, there is a great tradition of salting and curing, all guaranteed to keep a steady supply of meat throughout the year.

Those large Irish households have a reputation for hearty appetites, and it took a careful cook to extend a modest cut into a wholesome meal. The cleverness came through the use of grains and beans and, of course, basic vegetables, creating big soups and stews that would fill up even the most hungry of souls.

Lamb stew is probably Ireland's national dish, with every housewife having the best recipe around, but really it is a big, juicy steak that is still said to be the favorite by far. Many a man still looks forward to his Saturday night plate of a choice cut of beef.

Today, many of the old-fashioned dishes are creeping back into popularity. Spiced beef, slow braises, large roasts married naturally to carrots and barley, corned beef and cabbage—these dishes can be found on even upmarket menus. Is this just a trend following the resurgence of regional dishes? Or perhaps people are finally ready for wholesome, savory food again.

Grilled Lamb Shank
with Braised Fennel and Garlic

LAMB SHANKS HAVE BEEN ENJOYING A POPULAR REVIVAL WORLDWIDE. IT IS ABOUT TIME; WE'VE BEEN ENJOYING THESE SUCCULENT PIECES SINCE CHILDHOOD! THEY'RE AN ITEM NOT TO BE AFRAID OF, SINCE THEY ARE VERY EASY AND FORGIVING TO COOK. THIS DISH GOES EXTREMELY WELL WITH CHAMP (SEE PAGE 139). **Serves 4**

4 lamb shanks

2 fennel bulbs

2 whole garlic bulbs

vegetable oil

1 1/2 cups water

1 tablespoon freshly ground black pepper

Preheat the oven to 250 degrees F.

Trim the shanks of excess fat and saw off the knuckle. Trim and cut the fennel bulbs in half. Blanch the garlic bulbs in salted boiling water for 5 minutes, then remove from the heat. Drain and, when they are cool enough to handle, peel each clove.

In a large, heavy ovenproof pot, brown the shanks on all sides, adding a little vegetable oil if needed to prevent scorching. Add 1/2 cup of the water, cover, and place in the preheated oven for 1 hour. After 1 hour, turn the shanks and add the garlic cloves. After another 30 minutes, add the fennel bulbs, and cook for about 30 minutes longer, or until the shanks are tender. Finally, add the black pepper.

Remove from the oven and transfer the shanks, garlic, and fennel to a deep platter. Keep warm. Strain the juices into a small pan and add the remaining 1 cup water. Bring to a simmer over low heat and skim off the fat as it comes to the surface. When the sauce is free and clear, strain it back over the lamb shanks and serve.

Lambs' Liver and Sweetbreads
with Crispy Fried Onions and Lentils

THIS IS A RECIPE FOR CONVERTING FOLK WHO DON'T NORMALLY EAT OFFAL (INNARDS). FAMILIAR YET ZINGY, TASTY FLAVORS SEDUCE THEM—THEN THEY ARE HOOKED! IT CAN BE DONE WITH JUST LIVER OR SWEETBREADS. THE DISH IS INEXPENSIVE TO MAKE, TOO. **Serves 4**

To prepare the lentils, rinse them well and put them in a pan with the water. Bring to a boil and simmer for 5 minutes, skimming the scum that comes to the surface. Add the chopped vegetables, the bay leaf, thyme, and salt. Simmer for 20 minutes, then leave to cool to luke-warm. Stir in the vinaigrette.

Slice the large onion into very thin slices against the grain. Dredge lightly in flour. Heat oil in a deep-fat fryer or deep frying pan to 350 degrees F, or until a cube of bread turns golden within 1 minute. Add the onion slices and deep-fry for about 3 minutes, or until crisp and golden. Drain on kitchen paper, season lightly with salt, and keep in a warm place.

To cook the liver and sweetbreads, put the sweetbreads in a pan with plenty of cold water. Bring to a boil and simmer gently for 5 minutes. Drain the sweetbreads and refresh them in cold water. Peel off any tough membranous tissue and meat that is attached to the sweetbreads. Slice each sweetbread in half lengthwise. Season the pieces with salt and pepper. In a sauté pan, sauté the sweetbreads in a mixture of olive oil and butter over medium-high heat, turning as necessary. When they are brown and slightly crisp, remove from the pan and keep warm.

Wipe the pan and add some fresh oil and butter. Season the liver and then dredge lightly in flour. Cook the liver on each side for about 2 minutes for pink, or 3 minutes on each side for well done.

To serve, spoon the lentils onto warmed plates and heap a pile of the crisp onions at the base. Carefully present the liver and sweetbreads on top of the lentils.

---

1 large onion

all-purpose flour for dredging

vegetable oil for deep-frying

salt

1 pound lamb sweetbreads

salt and freshly ground black pepper

olive oil and unsalted butter for frying

1 1/2 pounds lambs' liver, sliced 1/2-inch thick

For the lentils:

rounded 1 cup green or brown lentils

2 1/2 cups water

2 tablespoons finely chopped onion

1 tablespoon finely chopped carrot

1 tablespoon finely chopped leek

1 bay leaf

a pinch of dried thyme

1 teaspoon salt

1/2 cup Vinaigrette Dressing (see page 177)

Noisettes of Lamb
with an Herb and Olive Crust

THIS TECHNIQUE CAN BE APPLIED TO FISH FILLETS JUST AS EASILY AS MEAT. IF YOU WANT TO MAKE IT A LITTLE SIMPLER, LEAVE OUT THE CHICKEN MOUSSE AND SIMPLY BRUSH THE LAMB WITH OLIVE TAPENADE OR MUSTARD AND THEN PRESS ON THE BREAD CRUMBS. **Serves 4**

1 saddle of lamb

2 tablespoons light olive oil

1 cup finely chopped mixed carrot, onion, and leek

4 1/2 cups Brown Chicken Stock (see page 178)

1 chicken breast, skinned and boned

1 egg white

1 cup whipping cream

1 tablespoon chopped fresh parsley

1 tablespoon chopped fresh rosemary

1 tablespoon chopped fresh thyme

1/2 cup black olives, pitted and finely chopped

1 garlic clove, finely chopped

1/2 cup coarse dried bread crumbs

2 tablespoons unsalted butter

Bone out the saddle of lamb so that you have 2 boneless loins. Reserve the bones. Cut each loin into 6 pieces. Lightly flatten each noisette with a heavy cleaver. Heat the olive oil in a heavy pan until smoking. Fry each noisette quickly on both sides so that they have a beautiful rich brown color. Allow to cool.

Chop the lamb bones roughly and brown in a heavy pan with the mixed chopped vegetables. Add the chicken stock and simmer for about 1 hour. Strain through a fine-mesh sieve, then return the liquid to the pan and boil to reduce to a sauce consistency. Keep warm.

Preheat the oven to 400 degrees F. Butter a baking dish large enough to accommodate the lamb noisettes in a single layer.

Puree the chicken breast and egg white in a food processor until smooth. Add the cream in a slow, steady stream and process until you have a smooth, homogeneous mixture. Add the parsley, rosemary, thyme, olives, and garlic and mix these in thoroughly. Spread each noisette with some of the chicken-olive mixture and dip the coated side into the bread crumbs. Place the noisettes in a prepared baking dish, crumb side up.

Put the baking dish into the preheated oven for 4 minutes. Turn each noisette upside down and bake for 1 minute longer. Serve with a little of the lamb sauce, reheating it if necessary.

Irish Stew

WHY IS IT THAT IRISH STEW IS SO FAMOUS? SURELY EVERY COUNTRY HAS IN ITS HISTORY A BASIC ONE-POT DISH. MAYBE IT IS JUST TOO TASTY AND WHOLESOME TO PASS UP. AT ANY RATE, THIS IS OUR CURRENT FAVORITE. **Serves 4**

Trim off the fatty film and excess fat from the lamb and cut the meat into large cubes. Place the lamb into a large, heavy pot with the water and a little salt. Bring to a boil, then skim off any scum from the surface. Simmer for 30 minutes.

Add half of the potatoes. Simmer for another 30 minutes, then stir up the pot quite vigorously to break up the potatoes. Add the remaining potatoes, carrots, leeks, onions, and thyme and simmer for about 30 minutes longer, or until the meat and all the vegetables are tender.

Add the parsley, cream, and butter. Reheat quickly and serve.

2 pounds boneless lamb shoulder or neck

5 cups water

salt

8 ounces potatoes, peeled and cut into coarse chunks

8 ounces carrots, peeled and thickly sliced

8 ounces leeks, well cleaned and thickly sliced

8 ounces baby onions, peeled

2 fresh thyme sprigs

1 cup fresh parsley leaves, blanched briefly and drained

1 cup whipping cream

1 tablespoon unsalted butter

OVERLEAF:

Left: Carpaccio of Beef with Roasted Eggplants and Balsamic Vinegar (page 100)

Right: Irish Stew

Carpaccio of Beef
with Roasted Eggplants and Balsamic Vinegar

WITH IRELAND'S LUSH PASTURES AND RICH FARMING TRADITIONS, THERE IS NO BETTER PLACE TO EAT RAW BEEF. TRY THIS VERSION OF A WORLD-FAMOUS CLASSIC. SERVE WITH CRUSTY BREAD. **Serves 4**

2 small eggplants

8 garlic cloves, unpeeled

1/2 cup light olive oil

10 ounces beef fillet

2 tablespoons coarse sea salt

1 teaspoon whole black peppercorns, cracked

1/2 cup balsamic vinegar

a few mixed salad leaves

1/2 cup shaved Parmesan cheese

Cut each eggplant into 4 thick slices. Gently crush the garlic cloves in their skins. Heat the light olive oil in a heavy frying pan over medium heat and add the eggplants and garlic. Cook together for 5 minutes on each side. Transfer the eggplant and garlic to a plate and allow to cool. Reserve the oil.

Thinly slice the beef fillet into 8 pieces. Gently pound the slices between 2 pieces of oiled plastic wrap until very thin. Try to slice the beef at an even thickness. Arrange these slices carefully on 4 plates.

To serve, sprinkle the beef with the sea salt and black peppercorns. Drizzle the beef slices with the balsamic vinegar, dividing it evenly. Carefully arrange the eggplants, garlic, and some salad leaves attractively around the beef. Sprinkle the shaved Parmesan over everything, and top with the reserved olive oil.

Sautéed Fillet of Beef
with Braised Oxtail, Mashed Potatoes, and Red Wine Sauce

HERE IS A RICH-MAN, POOR-MAN DISH. THERE IS NO DOUBT IN OUR MINDS THAT THE POOR OLD OXTAIL ELEVATES THIS PREPARATION A NOTCH OR TWO. TRY THE OXTAIL ON ITS OWN WITH PASTA OR MASHED POTATOES. **Serves 4**

Preheat the oven to 350 degrees F.

Trim the oxtails of all sinew and fat. If the oxtail is whole, cut into segments. Season with salt and pepper. In a large, heavy ovenproof pot, brown the oxtails in half of the butter, until nice and brown on all sides. Add the shallot, carrot, celery, and mushrooms, and cook, stirring, until lightly colored. Add the red wine and boil until reduced by half. Add the meat stock and Bouquet Garni and bring back to a boil. Skim off the scum. Cover and braise in the preheated oven for 2 hours.

Remove the oxtails from the pot, and flake the meat from the bones. Set aside in a warm place. Skim any fat off the cooking liquid, then pass it through a fine-mesh sieve into a stock and pass through a fine-mesh sieve in a saucepan. Heat to serving temperature; taste and adjust the seasoning. Keep hot.

In a heavy frying pan, sauté the beef fillets in the remaining butter for about 3 minutes each side. This timing depends on the size and shape of the fillets and how you prefer your meat. Set aside on a wire rack to rest for several minutes.

To assemble, place the potatoes in the center of warmed plates. Place the fillets on top. Carefully arrange the oxtail meat over the beef, and sprinkle on the scallions. Spoon the hot seasoned sauce around the potatoes.

1 pound oxtails

salt and freshly ground black pepper

4 tablespoons unsalted butter

1/3 cup finely chopped shallot

4 tablespoons finely chopped carrot

4 tablespoons finely chopped celery

1 ounce fresh mushrooms

3 1/2 cups dry red wine

4 cups meat stock

1 Bouquet Garni (see page 188)

4 beef fillets, about 6 ounces each, trimmed

mashed potatoes (1/2 recipe Champ, see page 139)

2 scallions, thinly sliced

Hot Smoked Fillet of Beef
with Arugula, Pine Nuts, and Roasted Peppers

THIS IS AN INTERESTING TECHNIQUE TO KNOW THAT'S A LITTLE FUSSY BUT FUN. IT JUST REQUIRES SOME PRACTICE. IDEALLY, A HOME SMOKER IS BEST, BUT SINCE MANY OF US DO NOT HAVE ONE, A COVERED WEBER-STYLE GRILL CAN BE USED. **Serves 4**

1 whole beef fillet, about 1 2/3 pounds, trimmed of fat and sinew

salt and whole black peppercorns, cracked

9 ounces arugula leaves

1/2 cup Vinaigrette Dressing (see page 177)

1/2 cup pine nuts, toasted

For the roasted peppers:

1 red bell pepper

1 yellow bell pepper

3 tablespoons light olive oil

To prepare the grill, build a small mound of charcoal in the charcoal pan of the grill. Very carefully light the fire. When the coals are covered with white ash, they will be very hot and ready for cooking.

When the fire is at this stage, brush the peppers with the oil and grill them for about 10 minutes until the skins are blistered and blackened, turning them frequently to ensure even cooking. Remove them from the heat and, when they are cool enough, peel off the skins. Halve and seed the peppers and cut into slices. Set aside.

Lay some water-soaked wood such as oak, applewood, or hickory on the top of the coals. Season the beef fillet generously with salt and peppercorns and place on the center of the grill rack. Place on the lid of the barbecue and let the meat cook and simultaneously smoke for about 45 minutes for rare beef, 1 1/2 hours for well done. Watch that the ashes are not too hot in the middle of the rack. If the fire is burning too quickly, slow this down by sprinkling a little water over it.

To serve, dress the arugula with vinaigrette and pile neatly at the top of warm plates. Slice the beef fillet, arrange below the salad, and sprinkle with pine nuts. Finally, place a few pepper slices at the bottom.

CHAPTER TEN

The Forest

The isle of Ireland was once a huge forest; mind you, that was a very long time ago. However, one can see how the damp climate is conducive to both the forests and their undergrowth. Nowadays, the hedgerows and wood margins, as well as the many forest parks, still offer up an overwhelming variety of wild food.

It is a shame that so much of it lies unused due to our general ignorance. Just what is out there? The native berries are perhaps the most obvious treasures that one would encounter if out on a forest hike. Over the summer months there are wild strawberries and wild cherries. As summer draws to an end, blackberries and bilberries (cousins to blueberries) are in great abundance. On the old Irish calendar, Fraughan Sunday was a day specially set aside for going out and picking the fraughan (bilberries). As autumn approaches, it is elderberries and rowanberries (the fruits of an ash tree). The choices simply make our cooks' heads spin.

The variety and quantity of wild mushrooms is beginning to draw more interest again as well. There are porcini (cèpes), chanterelles, and hedgehogs, to name a few. Remember though, if in doubt of a mushroom's identity, don't eat it.

Then there are the wild sorrel and nettles, popular since early Christian times. There are gorse and coltsfoot—did you even know that they were edible?—chamomile, wild marjoram, mint, juniper. The list goes on and on, simply waiting to be rediscovered. Perhaps with the steady growth in artisan food culture there will also be a revival of interest and appreciation in the unharvested cornucopia of produce that the forest can offer us.

Wild Mushroom Mousse
with a Ragoût of Sautéed Mushrooms

WE BELIEVE IN NATURAL, HEALTHY TEXTURES AND TASTES, SO THIS MOUSSE IS NOT TOO CREAMY OR RICH. IT IS A GOOD DISH FOR ENTERTAINING, AS THE MOUSSE CAN BE COOKED IN THE MORNING AND THEN GENTLY REHEATED FOR DINNER. **Serves 6** (V)

Preheat the oven to 275 degrees F. Butter 6 ramekins.

To make the mousse, brush or wipe away any dirt from the porcini and field mushrooms. Chop them roughly. Heat the butter in a large pan and sauté the chopped mushrooms with the shallot and garlic for about 8 minutes, or until the mushrooms are nice and soft and have lost any excess moisture. Add the cream and boil for about 2 minutes until it thickens slightly. Remove from the heat. Pour into a blender and puree until smooth. With the blender running, slowly add the whole eggs, the egg yolks, and salt and pepper to taste and blend for a further 10 seconds.

Fill the prepared ramekins with the mousse mixture, dividing it evenly. Cover each ramekin with a small square of aluminum foil. Place in a roasting pan and add hot water to reach halfway up the sides of the ramekins. Bake in the preheated oven for 40 minutes, or until the mousses are nicely set. Remove from the oven and set aside; keep warm.

To make the ragoût, pick through the wild mushrooms, trimming and scraping away any dirty or discolored pieces. Heat the oil in a large frying pan over high heat. When it is very hot, add the mushrooms and the butter. Fry gently for 3 to 4 minutes, or until the mushrooms are tender. Season with salt and pepper and turn into a colander to remove any excess liquid.

To serve, tip the mousses out onto warmed plates. Carefully surround with the sautéed mushrooms and sprinkle on the chives. Garnish each plate with a sprig of chervil.

For the mousse:

4 to 5 ounces fresh porcini mushrooms or 1 ounce dried

4 to 5 ounces fresh cremini or other brown field mushrooms

3 tablespoons unsalted butter

1 shallot, finely chopped

1 garlic clove, finely chopped

1 cup whipping cream

2 whole eggs

2 egg yolks

salt and freshly ground white pepper

For the ragoût:

9 ounces mixed fresh wild mushrooms such as chanterelles, porcini, and hedgehogs, in any combination

2 tablespoons olive oil

2 tablespoons unsalted butter

salt and freshly ground black pepper

To garnish:

2 tablespoons finely snipped fresh chives

6 fresh chervil sprigs

OVERLEAF:

Left: Blackberry Fool with Hazelnut Cookies (page 111)

Right: Chargrilled Porcini and Polenta with Arugula and Chili-Garlic Oil (page 109)

Wild Mushroom Ravioli
with a Mushroom Soy Jus

THIS VEGETARIAN DISH IS A GOURMET'S DELIGHT. IT HAS SIMPLICITY, CLEAR FLAVORS, AND A TWIST THAT DOESN'T CLASH OR INTERFERE WITH WHAT IS MOST IMPORTANT—TASTY MUSHROOM RAVIOLI! **Serves 4** Ⓥ

For the filling:

2 1/2 ounces shallots, chopped

4 to 5 ounces white portion of leek, finely chopped

1 garlic clove

1 tablespoon light olive oil

1 tablespoon unsalted butter

4 to 5 ounces fresh field or button mushrooms, sliced

4 to 5 ounces fresh shiitake mushrooms, sliced

2 1/2 ounces dried porcini mushrooms, soaked in hot water for 30 minutes, drained, and chopped

3/4 cup light cream

2/3 cup fine dried bread crumbs

For the mushroom soy jus:

3/4 cup vegetable stock

2 tablespoons mushroom soy sauce

1 1/2 teaspoons unsalted butter

9 ounces Ravioli Pasta Dough (see page 180)

1 egg yolk, lightly beaten

To garnish:

4 tablespoons finely snipped fresh chives

4 tablespoons julienned leek, blanched briefly and drained

To make the filling, fry the shallots, leek, and garlic with the oil and butter in a heavy frying pan over medium heat until they are soft. Add all the mushrooms, cover, and continue to cook until the mushrooms start to release their moisture. Remove the lid, add the cream, and simmer to reduce the juices until the mixture is quite dry. Remove from the heat and stir in the bread crumbs. Chop the mixture or process in a food processor until it has a pleasant, coarse texture. Set aside.

To make the jus, heat the vegetable stock and the mushroom soy sauce together in a small pan. When it comes to a boil, remove from the heat and stir in the butter. Set aside.

To make the ravioli, roll out the pasta dough as thinly as possible, or use the thinnest setting of your pasta machine. Cut out rounds with a cutter 3 to 4 inches in diameter, and carefully brush each one with some of the egg yolk. Place a spoonful of the filling in the center of each circle and fold over to form a half circle. Make sure that all the edges are sealed completely. Continue forming the half circles until you have 4 to 6 ravioli for each person, depending on the size of your circles and whether the dish is to be a starter or a main course portion.

Bring a large pot of salted water to a boil. Gently lower the ravioli into the boiling water and cook for about 3 minutes, or until they rise to the surface. Remove with a slotted spoon and serve immediately on warmed soup plates. Quickly reheat the mushroom soy jus and pour it over the ravioli. Garnish with the chives and the julienned leeks.

Chargrilled Porcini and Polenta
with Arugula and Chili-Garlic Oil

THIS IS A VERY ITALIAN DISH, THE TYPE OF PREPARATION YOU MIGHT HAVE HAD ON A TRIP TO ITALY YEARS AGO AND YOU STILL REMEMBER. WE'VE INCLUDED IT BECAUSE WE BELIEVE THAT IT TASTES JUST AS GOOD WHEN MADE WITH OUR LOCAL MUSHROOMS AND ARUGULA. **Serves 4**

Preheat the broiler or prepare a charcoal fire. To make the polenta, fry the onion in a heavy saucepan over medium heat with a little of the butter until soft and translucent. Add the water and bring to a boil. Gradually pour in the polenta, stirring all the time so that it remains smooth. Cook over medium heat for 4 to 5 minutes for instant polenta or 20 to 30 minutes for regular polenta, or until the polenta pulls away from the sides of the pan and no longer tastes gritty. Stir in the Parmesan and the remaining butter. Tip the cooked polenta into a buttered baking pan, cover with parchment paper, and let cool.

When the polenta is cool and firm, cut it into slices at least 1/2 inch thick and brush with the olive oil so that it is all ready for grilling.

To make the chili-garlic oil, chop the garlic, anchovies, and red pepper flakes with the salt. In a small pan, heat this mixture with the light olive oil for about 5 minutes, or until the garlic begins to soften. Allow this infusion to cool, then dilute it with the virgin olive oil.

To prepare the porcini, brush or wipe off any dirt and scrape the stems lightly with a sharp knife. Cut the larger mushrooms into a few slices and cut the smaller ones simply in half through the stem. Brush lightly with the olive oil and season with salt and pepper.

Place the mushrooms and polenta slices on a broiler pan or place on the grill rack. Broil or grill for 3 minutes. Turn over the polenta and mushrooms and cook for another 3 minutes.

Dress the arugula with a little of the chili-garlic oil. Arrange the mushrooms, polenta, and dressed arugula in a casual, rustic way on each of the 4 plates. Drizzle with the chili-garlic oil.

1 pound fresh porcini or any other boletus mushroom

about 1/2 cup light olive oil

salt and freshly ground white pepper

7 ounces arugula leaves

For the polenta:

1 onion, finely chopped

5 tablespoons unsalted butter, at room temperature

4 1/2 cups water

1 3/4 cups polenta

2/3 cup freshly grated Parmesan cheese

2 tablespoons olive oil

For the chili-garlic oil:

6 garlic cloves, peeled

4 anchovy fillets

1 tablespoon red pepper flakes

1/2 teaspoon salt

4 tablespoons light olive oil

2/3 cup virgin olive oil

Rice Pudding
with Fruits of the Forest Compote

RICE PUDDING IS A BRITISH CLASSIC. ANY MIXTURE OF BERRIES CAN BE USED FOR THE COMPOTE, AND THEIR SLIGHT TARTNESS MARRIES WELL WITH THE CREAMY PUDDING. **Serves 6 to 8** (V)

For the fresh fruit compote:

2/3 cup fresh red currants or black currants

1 cup blackberries

1 cup raspberries

2/3 to 3/4 cup superfine sugar

squeeze of lemon juice

For the rice pudding:

2/3 cup Arborio rice or other short-grain rice

4 1/2 cups milk or whipping cream (for a richer version), or half milk and half cream, or as needed

scant 1/2 cup sugar

1 tablespoon fresh lemon zest

1 vanilla bean, split lengthwise

3 egg yolks, lightly beaten

3 egg whites

4 tablespoons superfine sugar

To make the compote, put all the berries in a small bowl, add the superfine sugar, and leave them to macerate for at least an hour. Add a squeeze of lemon juice and set aside.

Meanwhile, preheat the oven to 300 degrees F.

To make the pudding, in a heavy baking dish, combine the rice, 4 1/2 cups milk and/or cream, sugar, lemon zest, and the vanilla bean. Cover and place in the preheated oven and cook for about an hour, depending on the brand and type of rice used. During this time, check the rice several times, adding more milk as necessary to keep it moist and loose. When the rice is tender to the bite, remove from the oven and allow to cool slightly. Leave the oven set at 300 degrees F.

Stir the egg yolks into the pudding. Whip the whites until firm and glossy, adding the sugar toward the end of the whipping time. Fold into the rice mixture. Generously butter a baking dish and pour the rice mixture into it. Place in a roasting pan and add hot water to reach halfway up the sides of the dish. Return the pudding to the oven for 30 to 45 minutes longer, or until the top is nice and golden brown.

To serve, scoop out the rice pudding onto warmed plates, and place a generous dollop of the berry compote on the side.

Blackberry Fool
with Hazelnut Cookies

REMEMBER THE OLD SAYING "THE SIMPLE THINGS ARE ALWAYS THE BEST"? WITH THE SIMPLICITY OF A FOOL AND GORGEOUS FRUIT FOR FREE, EVERYONE SHOULD BE MAKING THIS DISH! THE TASTY COOKIES KEEP VERY WELL IN AN AIRTIGHT CONTAINER. **Serves 4** (V)

To make the fool, reserve a handful of blackberries for the garnish and puree the remainder with sugar to taste in a blender. Pass through a fine-mesh sieve into a bowl. The resulting puree should be thick. Add the lemon juice, then taste and adjust the flavoring.

Whisk the cream until soft peaks form. Beat the mascarpone cheese until softened, then whisk the two gently together. Do not overbeat. Finally, pour off two-thirds of the puree into a bowl and fold this cream mixture into it. Reserve the remaining puree.

In a sundae dish or wineglass, place a few of the reserved blackberries tossed in a spoonful of the reserved puree. Fill the glass halfway with the creamy mixture. Place a thin layer of the puree on top of this layer before filling the glass with more creamy mixture. Fill the other dishes in the same way. Cover and chill for at least 2 hours to firm up the mixture.

Preheat the oven to 350 degrees F. To make the cookies, place the hazelnuts on a baking sheet. Toast in the preheated oven for about 10 minutes, or until the skins darken and are beginning to loosen. Remove from the oven, wrap the warm nuts in a towel, and rub vigorously between your palms to loosen the skins. Nearly all the skins should flake off fully. Chop and set aside.

Butter the baking sheet. In a bowl, beat together the sugar and butter until light and fluffy. Add the eggs and vanilla and mix until well. In another bowl, sift together the flour, baking soda, and baking powder. Fold the flour mixture into the butter-egg mixture. Finally, fold in the nuts. Drop spoonfuls onto the baking sheet, leaving space to allow for spreading. Bake in the preheated oven for about 8 minutes, or until golden brown. Transfer to a rack to cool.

Garnish with the reserved berries and serve with the cookies.

For the fool:

2 3/4 cups blackberries

1/3 to 1/2 cup sugar

juice of 1 lemon

1/2 cup whipping cream

4 tablespoon mascarpone cheese or 4 additional tablespoons whipping cream

For the hazelnut cookies:

1 cup hazelnuts

2 cups superfine sugar

1 cup plus 2 tablespoons (9 ounces) unsalted butter, at room temperature

2 eggs

1 teaspoon vanilla extract

2 cups all-purpose flour

1 teaspoon baking soda

1 teaspoon baking powder

Elderflower and Champagne Sorbet

EVERY TIME PAUL TASTES THIS SORBET, HE REMEMBERS THAT HE LOVES THE TASTE OF ELDERFLOWERS. A COOL, REFRESHING SORBET IS THE PERFECT CARRIER FOR ITS MUSKY FRUIT FLOWERS. WE ALWAYS USE AN ICE CREAM MACHINE, AS IT GUARANTEES THE BEST RESULTS. **Serves 6**

1 1/4 cups Sugar Syrup (see page 188)

grated zest and juice of 1 lemon

4 big bunches of fresh elderflowers or 1 1/2 ounces dried

1 1/4 cups Champagne

1 tablespoon egg white

fresh mint sprigs or berries

Place the Sugar Syrup in a pan and bring to a boil. Add the lemon zest and the elderflowers and set aside to infuse for 20 minutes. Strain through a fine-mesh sieve and leave to cool.

Add the Champagne and lemon juice to the cooled syrup and taste for flavor. It may require a little more lemon juice. Place in an ice cream machine with the egg white and freeze according to the manufacturer's instructions. If you do not have a machine, spoon into a freezer tray and freeze until firm, whisking every 30 minutes to break up the ice crystals.

Serve in well-chilled glasses as a refresher between courses or as a light dessert. Garnish with a sprig of mint or perhaps a few berries.

CHAPTER ELEVEN

The Herb Garden

As with other foods, herbs and their uses have been exchanged among countries since the spread of civilization. Used for medicinal or culinary purposes, fresh herbs have been part of the Irish countryside for centuries.

Many of the great estates of the past had a sizable herb garden. In fact, one can still see huge bushes of rosemary, lavender, thyme, and mint growing in great profusion in the gardens of the National Trust houses all over the country.

Nowadays, almost every county can boast of at least half a dozen organic growers, and as demand for organic herbs continues to increase, so will supply.

Fresh herbs can be quite intimidating at first, especially for anyone who was raised with only those little jars of dried, store-bought ones in the house. But the only way to get one's feet wet is to plunge right in. Start with the most common herbs, and then as confidence grows, branch out and discover other more unusual ones. There is an endless variety to choose from. Handfuls of chopped fresh parsley can deliver just the right finish to many dishes. Try strewing some over omelets, salads, or soups. Use fresh sage the next time you make a stuffing, add a sprig or two of fresh thyme to flavor a meat roast or stew, or throw together your own fresh mint sauce for that Sunday roast of lamb. You will experience a different level of taste and sensation with fresh herbs.

The storing of fresh herbs is simple but important. Wrap them separately in paper towels and then place inside unsealed plastic bags. Keep these in the vegetable crisper of your refrigerator. They should last several days at least, depending on their condition when you purchased them.

Of course, another alternative is to start your own little stock pile of fresh plants. Most will live quite happily in a pot on the kitchen windowsill and need very little attention other than water and sunlight. There's a multitude of books on the market about cultivating herbs.

Fresh herbs really do justify themselves and any time devoted to learning about them will be rewarded. Once you have developed a taste for them, your cooking will never be the same again.

Chervil and Potato Soup

SERVE THIS LOVELY SOUP IN EARLY AUTUMN WHEN CHERVIL AND POTATOES ARE AT THEIR BEST. THE RECIPE CAN BE VARIED WITH THE ADDITION OF CHICKEN, SMOKED SALMON, MUSHROOMS, OR OTHER FAVORITE INGREDIENTS. **Serves 8** (V)

Melt the butter in a large saucepan over low heat and fry the onions with a little salt and pepper for 10 minutes, or until translucent. Meanwhile, strip the leaves from the chervil stems and finely chop the stems. Reserve the leaves. Add the stems, potatoes, Bouquet Garni, and the chicken stock to the pan and bring to a boil. Simmer for 20 minutes.

Remove from the heat and allow to cool for 15 minutes. Discard the Bouquet Garni. Add the chervil leaves and puree in a blender in batches. Pass through a fine-mesh sieve into a clean saucepan. Check the seasoning, adding salt and white pepper as necessary.

Heat the soup gently without allowing it to boil. Ladle into warmed bowls and garnish with a dollop of cream and a sprig of chervil.

4 tablespoons unsalted butter

12 ounces onions, chopped

salt and freshly ground white pepper

1 large bunch fresh chervil, about 5 ounces

12 ounces floury potatoes, peeled and diced

1 Bouquet Garni (see page 188)

5 cups chicken stock or water

7 tablespoons whipping cream, whipped to soft peaks

fresh chervil sprigs

Artichoke Ravioli
with Basil Pesto

BASIL PESTO IS ONE OF THOSE FOODS JUST BURSTING WITH FLAVOR. ITS SENSUAL AROMA LIFTS ANYTHING IT'S SERVED WITH TO DIZZYING FLAVOR HEIGHTS. **Serves 4** (ⓥ)

For the pasta dough:

4 2/3 cups all-purpose flour

4 eggs

5 egg yolks

salt

3 tablespoons vegetable oil

2 tablespoons water

For the filling:

2 large artichokes

1 tablespoon unsalted butter

1 tablespoon chopped onion

1 garlic clove

2 ounces fresh button mushrooms, sliced

2 tablespoons fine dried bread crumbs

salt and freshly ground black pepper

1 egg, lightly beaten

1 tablespoon olive oil

To make the pasta dough, combine all the ingredients in a bowl or food processor and beat or process until they come together in a smooth mass. As flours vary, more water or more flour may need to be added until the consistency is right.

Roll out the dough very thin by hand on a floured work surface or on a pasta machine. The dough will be a little softer and more pliable than a normal pasta dough. This is needed so that it can be shaped around the filling. Lay each sheet of pasta on a tray, stacking them with a sheet of plastic wrap between the layers. A damp towel over the top will help prevent the sheets from drying out. Set aside.

To make the filling, carefully trim off all the outside leaves from the artichokes with a very sharp knife until you are left with only the pale artichoke heart. Simmer the artichokes in boiling water for about 20 minutes, or until tender. Leave to cool in the cooking liquid. Remove the hairy choke from the center of the artichokes and set one artichoke aside for later. Chop the other artichoke roughly and set aside for the moment.

In a pan, melt the butter and fry the onion and garlic until soft and lightly browned. Add the sliced mushrooms and cook until most of the moisture has evaporated and the mushrooms are well cooked. Tip the mushroom mixture into a food processor and pulse until you have a coarse mixture, or chop finely. Add the chopped artichoke, bread crumbs, and salt and pepper to taste and pulse again or mix together just to reincorporate all the ingredients. Scrape the mixture into a bowl. When it is cool, add the egg.

To make the basil pesto, put the pine nuts, garlic, and olive oil into a blender and process until fairly smooth. Add the basil leaves,

Parmesan, and salt and pepper to taste and process again until the leaves are completely incorporated.

To assemble the ravioli, cut the pasta into 2-inch squares and lay them out on a work surface. Brush the surface of half of the squares with the beaten egg, then spoon a dollop of the filling onto the center of each square. Carefully cover these with the remaining squares, pressing gently to seal all the edges.

Slice the remaining artichoke into small pieces and sauté in the olive oil until lightly browned.

Bring a large pot of salted water to a boil. Gently lower the ravioli into the boiling water and cook for 2 minutes, or until they are just tender and rise to the top. Using a slotted spoon, lift out the ravioli, draining well. Serve the ravioli on warmed plates, scatter on the slices of sautéed artichoke, and drizzle the basil pesto generously over the top.

Note: This will make more dough than is required for this recipe. Any remaining dough can be frozen.

For the basil pesto:

4 tablespoons pine nuts

3 garlic cloves

1/2 cup virgin olive oil

4 1/2 to 5 cups loosely packed fresh basil leaves

4 tablespoons freshly grated Parmesan cheese

salt and freshly ground black pepper

1 egg, lightly beaten, for sealing ravioli

Sorrel Soufflé
with Fresh Tomato Sauce

SORREL HAS A GREAT AFFINITY FOR EGGS, ITS SHARPNESS BALANCING AND COUNTERACTING THE RICHNESS OF THE YOLKS. THIS IS A GREAT TOMATO SAUCE TO KNOW AS IT IS SIMPLE AND QUICK. **Serves 4** (V)

For the soufflé:

4 tablespoons unsalted butter

1 pound sorrel, trimmed and finely chopped

3 eggs, separated

4 ounces white bread, crusts removed, soaked in milk, squeezed dry, and chopped

salt and freshly ground white pepper

4 tablespoons freshly grated Parmesan cheese

For the tomato sauce:

2 tablespoons finely chopped shallot

1/2 cup (4 ounces) plus 1 tablespoon unsalted butter, diced

1 tablespoon tomato paste

6 plum tomatoes, peeled, seeded, and chopped

salt and freshly ground black pepper

Preheat the oven to 375 degrees F. Butter 4 soufflé ramekins each of which will hold a scant 1 cup.

To make the tomato sauce, in a nonreactive frying pan, fry the shallot in the 1 tablespoon butter over medium heat for 3 minutes. Do not allow to color. Add the tomato paste and chopped tomatoes and cook for about 5 minutes, or until the tomato pieces have wilted and the sauce is just starting to thicken. Whisk in the diced butter 1 tablespoon at a time. Season with salt and pepper and set aside. Keep warm.

To make the soufflé, melt the butter in a nonreactive frying pan and cook the sorrel over low heat for about 3 minutes, or until it is completely soft. Remove from the heat. Beat the egg yolks in a small bowl, add to the sorrel, and mix well. Add the soaked bread and mix thoroughly. Season with salt and white pepper.

Coat the bottom and sides of the prepared ramekins lightly with the Parmesan cheese. In a bowl, combine the egg whites and a pinch of salt and beat until very stiff but not grainy. Fold into the sorrel mixture just until combined and transfer to the ramekins, dividing evenly.

Bake in the preheated oven for about 15 minutes, or until well risen and nicely browned on top. Just before the soufflés are ready, gently reheat the sauce. Serve the soufflés immediately with the fresh tomato sauce on the side.

Roasted Sea Bass
with a Parsley and Caper Sauce

SEA BASS IS A PROTECTED SPECIES IN SOUTHERN IRELAND, AND IT IS RARELY SEEN IN NORTHERN WATERS. IF YOU ARE LUCKY ENOUGH TO CATCH ONE YOURSELF, TREAT THIS SPECIAL FISH WITH RESPECT AND COOK IT SIMPLY, AS IS DONE HERE. SERVE WITH STEAMED NEW POTATOES AND A GREEN SALAD. **Serves 4**

Check the sea bass fillet for any errant bones and scales, and divide into 4 equal portions. Season the fillets generously with salt and pepper and lightly dredge in the flour.

Heat 2 tablespoons of the olive oil in a large frying pan (preferably nonstick) over medium heat and sauté the sea bass for about 5 minutes on each side.

While the sea bass is cooking, grind the parsley, capers, anchovies, and garlic in a mortar with a pestle or in a food processor. Finally, when it is fairly well mixed together, add the mustard, lemon juice, and the remaining virgin olive oil. Season with pepper and check for salt.

To serve, spoon some of the sauce onto each of the warmed plates and carefully set the sea bass on top.

1 1/3 pounds sea bass fillet with skin intact

salt and freshly ground white pepper

3/4 cup all-purpose flour

1/2 cup plus 1 tablespoon virgin olive oil

3 tablespoons chopped fresh parsley

2 tablespoons drained capers

4 anchovy fillets

1 garlic clove, chopped

1 teaspoon Dijon mustard

1 tablespoon fresh lemon juice

Rack of Pork
with Grilled Vegetables and Herbes de Provence

USE A SELECTION OF VEGETABLES IN SEASON FOR THIS DISH, MAKING SURE THEY ARE OF THE BEST QUALITY.

Serves 4

1 rack of pork, about 2 pounds
with 4 or 5 rib bones

2 tablespoons sea salt

1 tablespoon freshly ground
black pepper

1 cup light olive oil

For the herbes de Provence:

2 tablespoons chopped
fresh parsley

1 tablespoon chopped fresh thyme

1 tablespoon chopped fresh
rosemary

1 teaspoon chopped fresh sage

1 teaspoon dried oregano

2 bay leaves, crushed

For the dressing:

1 cup virgin olive oil

juice of 1 lemon

1 teaspoon salt

1 teaspoon whole black
peppercorns, cracked

For the vegetables:

about 2 pounds mixed vegetables
such as eggplants, zucchini, red
onion, mushrooms, leeks, carrots,
and/or potatoes, in any
combination

1/2 cup olive oil

salt and freshly ground
black pepper

Trim any skin from the rack of pork and thoroughly remove the meat from between the bones to expose them. Mix together all the ingredients for the herbes de Provence. Rub the salt, black pepper, and 2 tablespoons of the mixed herbs into the pork rack, and then cover and refrigerate for at least 4 hours or as long as 8 hours.

About 1 hour before serving, prepare a charcoal fire or preheat the broiler. Take the pork out of the refrigerator, drain off any juices, and lightly pat dry. When the barbecue or broiler is hot, drizzle a little olive oil over the pork and put it over medium-hot coals or several inches from the broiler heat. Cook for about 30 minutes, turning and basting with the olive oil from time to time.

Meanwhile, place all the ingredients for the dressing in a small bowl and whisk together thoroughly. Add 2 tablespoons of the herb mixture and allow to stand while you prepare the vegetables.

Cut the vegetables into attractive shapes and sizes but make sure that they are not so small that they will fall through the grill rack into the coals or be difficult to handle in the broiler. Toss the vegetables in the olive oil and sprinkle with the remaining herbes de Provence and a little salt and pepper.

When the pork is ready, transfer it to a platter and let rest for 5 to 10 minutes. Immediately start cooking the vegetables on the hottest part of the grill or in the broiler. Watch them very carefully, turning them once or twice before removing them to a warmed plate.

To serve, carve the rack of pork into 4 large chops. Arrange enough vegetables for each person on each plate, place the cutlet in the center, drizzle the whole plate with the herb dressing, and serve.

Warm Parsley Salad
with White Beans and Tongue

THIS DISH IS BEST MADE WITH YOUNG PARSLEY. THE CURLY AND FLAT-LEAF VARIETIES WILL WORK EQUALLY WELL. **Serves 4**

Place the beans in a bowl and pour enough water over them to cover generously. Let them soak overnight. Rinse the beans, and place them in a saucepan. Add water to cover by 3/4 inch, bring to a boil, reduce the heat to low, and simmer gently for 1 hour.

Add the onion, carrot, bay leaf, and salt and continue to simmer for 1 hour, or until the beans are beginning to burst. The timing will depend on the age of the beans; new crop beans will cook more quickly. Remove from the heat and allow to cool for about 5 minutes. Add the parsley leaves, vinaigrette, and the pepper and mix well.

To serve, spoon the bean and parsley mixture onto warmed plates, and scatter the tongue over the top.

3/4 cup dried small white beans, rinsed

2 tablespoons chopped onion

2 tablespoons chopped carrot

1/2 bay leaf

salt

leaves from 1 bunch fresh parsley

6 tablespoons Vinaigrette Dressing (see page 177)

freshly ground black pepper

9 ounces cooked beef tongue, sliced and then cut into 3/4-inch batons

OVERLEAF:

Left: Fruit Gâteau with Lemon Balm (page 124)

Right: Rack of Pork with Grilled Vegetables and Herbes de Provence (page 120)

Fruit Gâteau
with Lemon Balm

THIS MAKES FOR A DELIGHTFULLY LIGHT DESSERT, AS REFRESHING AS A SORBET ON THE PALATE YET RICHER IN TEXTURE AND APPEARANCE. IT COULD JUST AS EASILY BE MADE IN A TERRINE OR LOAF PAN AND THEN SLICED INTO PORTIONS. **Serves 6** Ⓥ

1/2 bottle dry Muscat wine

1 1/4 cups Sugar Syrup (see page 188)

1 bunch fresh lemon balm

4 large grapefruits

8 navel oranges

2 packages (1 tablespoon each) unflavored gelatin, softened in 1/4 cup cold water for about 3 minutes, or 8 leaves gelatin, soaked in cold water for 10 minutes

For the sauce:

1 1/4 cups fresh orange juice, strained

2/3 cup superfine sugar

1 1/2 tablespoons arrowroot or potato flour

3 tablespoons water

2 tablespoons grenadine syrup

fresh lemon balm or sprig of mint

Combine the wine, Sugar Syrup, and half of the lemon balm leaves in a large saucepan over medium heat and simmer for about 20 minutes to infuse the liquid with the lemon balm.

Meanwhile, cut away the skin and pith from the grapefruits and oranges. Neatly slice out the segments, cutting on either side of each with a knife to free them completely from the membrane. Work over a bowl as you do this, in order to catch the juices and segments. It is very important to lay the segments out on a cotton towel or paper towels now to let the individual segments dry. If you don't do this, the jelly will have trouble adhering to the segments and the whole thing may fall apart when you unmold it.

Add the softened gelatin or gelatin leaves to the infusion and stir until well dissolved. Strain through a very fine-mesh sieve. Allow to cool to room temperature, but it must still be pourable.

Grease 6 little cups or molds with nonstick cooking spray. Pour just enough of the infusion into each one to cover the base to a depth of about 1/8 inch. Carefully lay 2 or 3 leaves of lemon balm onto this layer. Bear in mind that when presented, the bottom of the mold will be on top, so place the leaves in upside down, with the vein side facing up.

Lay the orange and grapefruit segments on the bases, alternating the two to provide a juxtaposition of the colors. Place them in rather tightly, not pressing them down or in, just making them fit snugly together. Ladle or pour in the infusion to cover the fruits, letting it fill all the gaps. Gently tap the mold once or twice on the countertop to remove any air bubbles, and fill up each mold to the rim. Cover and place in the refrigerator for at least 2 hours, or until the molds are set completely.

To make the sauce, combine the orange juice and sugar in a small pan and bring to a boil over medium-high heat. Mix the arrowroot or potato flour to a smooth paste with the water, then stir it into the pan and return to a boil. Let simmer for 1 minute, just to ensure that the arrowroot or potato flour is well dissolved. Remove from the heat and strain through a fine-mesh sieve. Add the grenadine and chill in the refrigerator. The chilled sauce should not be too thick in consistency, yet not too runny either.

Unmold each little gâteau onto a plate by running a very sharp knife around the edge of the mold and, if necessary, quickly dipping the mold into an inch or so of very hot water. This slightly melts the jelly, releasing the edges and bottom. Surround with the chilled sauce and garnish with a sprig of lemon balm or mint.

Red Wine and Fresh Thyme Poached Figs

TO PREPARE FRUITS WITH A "SAVORY" HERB IS NOT AT ALL A NEW IDEA: PEAR AND BASIL IS A WELL-KNOWN EXAMPLE. JEANNE FEELS THAT FRESH THYME DRAWS OUT THE "TOBACCO-EY" ESSENCE OF THE FIGS, ENHANCING THE DEEP, EARTHY FLAVOR. **Serves 4** (V)

Place the port and red wine in a wide saucepan and bring to a boil. Continue to boil until the liquid has reduced by half. Add the Sugar Syrup, lemon, thyme, and vanilla bean and return to a boil. Gently place the figs in a single layer in the saucepan, and cover with parchment paper. Simmer over a gentle heat for 5 minutes, and remove from the heat.

Using a slotted spoon, transfer the figs, thyme, and lemon to a bowl and cover them. Meanwhile, reduce the liquid over high heat by half. Pour the concentrated poaching liquid back over the figs, let cool, cover, and let steep overnight in the refrigerator. If desired, the liquid can again be reduced to a thick, syrupy consistency that would coat the back of a spoon. Don't put the thyme or lemon in during this reduction, as their flavors could become too strong.

To serve, place 3 figs on each serving plate. Serve crème fraîche or ice cream. Garnish with a few almonds, if desired.

1 1/2 cups ruby port

1 1/2 cups red wine

3 cups Sugar Syrup (see page 188)

1/2 lemon

4 fresh thyme sprigs

1/2 vanilla bean, split lengthwise

12 fresh ripe figs

To serve and garnish:

crème fraîche, or vanilla or almond ice cream

sliced or toasted almonds (optional)

The Vegetable Garden

Vegetables in their own right must be, by tradition, one of the most neglected foods in Ireland. They constitute by far the most varied and abundant source of nourishment, yet have been relegated to mere accompaniment status for far too long. Happily, things are now changing, slowly but surely. The widespread habit of holidaying on the Continent, as well as the Europeans coming to Ireland for their holidays, have helped open the eyes of the general public over the last twenty years or so.

Historically, it was only the great estates with their walled gardens that delved into growing various vegetables, experimenting with varieties and so on. The average farm may have grown a few spuds, perhaps some rutabagas and cabbage, maybe even some leeks, but on the whole the plantings were very basic. Part of the problem lies in the climate. The growing season's late start and early finish, the dampness, and the fact that the soil is heavy in many parts of the country all contribute to growing conditions that are less than ideal. Paul finds, though, that those vegetables cultivated locally in season do have a superb flavor due to the slow and natural growing. In fact, he claims that they are as good in quality as any of those we have bought in London, Australia, or even California. The developing interest in vegetables will hopefully encourage more growers to overcome these regional difficulties.

In general, there is a definite lack of knowledge of vegetables and ways to prepare and cook them. People have a tendency to overcook them, draining away flavor, texture, and nutritious value. Personally, we find great inspiration in vegetables, their variety and their natural seasons. Taking each harvest's bounty, the options are endless. One can boil or steam, panfry or deep-fry, bake or braise, batter or stuff. Obviously, different vegetables suit different techniques better than others, so just remember to treat each one with that in mind. Eating a wide variety ensures a healthy body, whether there is also meat in the diet or not.

Let the humble vegetable take center stage on your dinner plate. The more you cook with them, the more you will grow to appreciate their versatility and flavors.

Trio of Stuffed Vegetables

STUFFED VEGETABLES ARE VERSATILE. THEY MAKE GREAT STARTERS OR SIDE DISHES, AND HERE THREE HAVE BEEN PUT TOGETHER FOR A SUPERB VEGETARIAN MAIN COURSE. **Serves 2** ⓥ

Artichoke Stuffed with Creamed Eggplant

2 tablespoons olive oil

2 tablespoons white wine vinegar

4 1/2 cups water

1 tablespoon salt

2 medium artichokes

For the filling:

1 medium eggplant

salt and freshly ground white pepper

1/2 cup plus 1 tablespoon olive oil

1 tablespoon unsalted butter

5 ounces fresh shiitake mushrooms, trimmed

1 garlic clove, finely chopped

1 cup whipping cream

1 tablespoon chopped fresh parsley (optional)

Mix together the oil, vinegar, water, and salt in a saucepan. This is the cooking liquid. Carefully trim all the outside leaves from the artichokes with a very sharp knife until you are left with only the pale green artichoke hearts. Trim the stems even with the bottoms so the artichokes will stand upright. Add them to the pan, bring to a simmer, and cook for about 20 minutes, or until they are tender. Allow them to cool in the cooking liquid.

To make the filling, trim and chop the eggplant into 1/2-inch squares. Season with salt and pepper. Fry gently in the olive oil until golden brown and quite soft to the touch. Drain in a sieve.

Melt the butter and fry the mushrooms and garlic with a little salt and pepper. When the mushrooms are soft, add the cream and the eggplant squares and simmer for 3 to 5 minutes, or until the cream thickens.

When the artichokes are cool, remove the hairy chokes from the center with a small spoon. Heap the filling into each artichoke heart. Top with the chopped parsley, if you like, for some color.

Tomato Stuffed with Spinach

Trim a 1/4-inch-thick slice off the top of each tomato and carefully scoop out the pulp with a teaspoon. (Reserve the pulp for another use). Pick over and wash the spinach, removing any tough stems. Peel the garlic clove and skewer it onto the tines of a kitchen fork.

Heat the butter in a frying pan until it is golden brown. Add the spinach all at once. Stir immediately with the "garlic fork," add the nutmeg and salt and pepper to taste, and continue cooking for 2 to 4 minutes, or until the spinach is bright green and quite tender but not shapeless.

Drain off and discard any excess moisture from the spinach, then pile it into the tomatoes. Top with the crushed croutons or bread crumbs.

2 ripe, thick-fleshed tomatoes

4 to 5 ounces spinach

1 garlic clove

2 tablespoons unsalted butter

a pinch of freshly grated nutmeg

salt and freshly ground black pepper

finely crushed croutons or fine dried bread crumbs

Zucchini Stuffed with Ratatouille

Cut the whole zucchini in half lengthwise. Scoop out the flesh from each half to make a boat shape with sturdy sides. Blanch the zucchini halves in boiling water for 1 minute, then refresh in cold water and drain well. Finely dice the flesh and measure it; add more diced zucchini as needed to measure 1 cup.

In a frying pan, fry the onion and garlic in a little of the olive oil until soft. Fry the diced zucchini, eggplant, and red pepper separately in olive oil, draining each of them on paper towels to absorb excess oil. Carefully mix all the fried ingredients together in a bowl and season with salt and pepper. Pile into the zucchini boats.

Preheat the oven to 350 degrees F.

Put all the stuffed vegetables on a baking sheet and warm them in the preheated oven for about 10 minutes. Present a trio of each on separate plates. Garnish with fresh herbs.

1 beautiful zucchini, 5 to 6 inches long

1 small onion, finely chopped

1 garlic clove, crushed

1 cup olive oil

1 cup finely diced eggplant

1 small red bell pepper, finely diced

salt and freshly ground black pepper

fresh herbs of choice for garnishing all the vegetables

OVERLEAF:

Left: Trio of Stuffed Vegetables (pages 128-129)

Center: Asparagus and Wild Mushroom Bruschetta (page 133)

Right: Champ (page 139)

Warm Salad of Grilled Vegetables
with Parmesan and Balsamic Vinegar

THIS SUMMER DISH WAS INSPIRED ORIGINALLY BY THE EXCELLENT PRODUCE WE USED TO WORK WITH IN CALIFORNIA. THE FUNNY THING IS THAT IT TASTES JUST AS GOOD IN IRELAND WITH OUR OWN WONDERFUL, LOCAL SUMMER VEGETABLES. **Serves 6** (V)

1 red bell pepper

1 yellow bell pepper

7 tablespoons light olive oil

1 zucchini

1 eggplant

1 artichoke

1 red onion

3 small leeks, split lengthwise and well cleaned

6 large fresh mushrooms

salt and freshly ground black pepper

a few mixed salad leaves

7 tablespoons virgin olive oil

4 tablespoons balsamic vinegar

4-ounce wedge Parmesan cheese, shaved with a vegetable peeler

1 tablespoon chopped fresh thyme

1 tablespoon chopped fresh parsley

1 tablespoon whole black peppercorns, cracked

To prepare the vegetables, rub the peppers with a little light olive oil and roast them under a very hot broiler (or in a very hot oven) until the skins blacken and blister. Peel and seed each pepper, then slice each one into 6 pieces.

Slice the zucchini and eggplant into 1/2-inch-thick slices and drizzle lightly with light olive oil.

Carefully trim all the outside leaves from the artichoke with a very sharp knife until you are left with only the pale green artichoke heart. Cut the onion and the artichoke heart into 6 wedges and cut the choke away from the artichoke wedges. Blanch the onion wedges and the leeks in a pan of salted boiling water for 2 minutes each and refresh them under cold water.

Preheat the broiler. Arrange the vegetables on broiler pans according to their cooking times and brush them lightly with light olive oil. Season with salt and pepper. Broil the vegetables until just cooked. The peppers and the artichoke will take only 1 to 2 minutes, while the mushrooms, onion, zucchini, and eggplant will take about 5 minutes each.

To serve, arrange the vegetables attractively on the plates and place a few salad leaves in the center of each arrangement. Drizzle with the virgin olive oil and the balsamic vinegar. Sprinkle with the Parmesan, herbs, and black pepper.

Asparagus and Wild Mushroom Bruschetta

THIS MAY NOT BE A LOCAL DISH, BUT YOU CAN GROW GREAT ASPARAGUS IN IRELAND, AND WE HAVE PLENTY OF WILD MUSHROOMS. BRUSCHETTA IS A PEASANT-STYLE ITALIAN DISH THAT THE IRISH REALLY ENJOY. THERE ARE PLENTY OF WAYS YOU CAN VARY THE DISH TO SUIT YOUR OWN TASTE. YOU CAN USE PARMESAN AS A GARNISH, FOR EXAMPLE, GRILL THE BREAD AND ASPARAGUS FOR EXTRA FLAVOR, OR SUBSTITUTE CHICKEN, PORK, OR FENNEL FOR THE ASPARAGUS. ANY LEFTOVER MUSHROOMS CAN BE FROZEN. **Serves 4** Ⓥ

To prepare the mushrooms, in a large frying pan, fry the onion and garlic in the oil until soft and translucent. Add the fresh and dried mushrooms and cook for about 10 minutes. Allow the mixture to cool a little before chopping or processing in a food processor until coarsely chopped. It should not be too fine; there should be texture and shape left in the mushrooms. Season generously with salt and pepper and a little of the truffle or olive oil.

To make the bruschetta, preheat the broiler. Brush each side of the bread slices with a little olive oil. If you like garlic, you may want to rub each slice with a peeled clove as well. Toast under the hot broiler until crisp.

To cook the asparagus, break off any very tough parts of the spears. If the skin is tough, peel the spears carefully. Cook in salted boiling water for 4 to 8 minutes, depending on size. Drain carefully and set aside.

To serve, spread the hot mushroom mixture generously on the toasted bread and set in the middle of warmed plates. Top with the asparagus spears and drizzle the whole thing with the remaining truffle or olive oil. Garnish with sautéed mushrooms, a few salad leaves, or sprigs of parsley or chervil, if desired.

For the mushrooms:

1 cup chopped onion

3 garlic cloves, crushed

1/2 cup olive oil

1 pound fresh button mushrooms, roughly chopped

2 1/2 ounces dried porcini mushrooms, soaked for 30 minutes in hot water and drained

salt and freshly ground black pepper

4 tablespoons truffle oil or olive oil

For the bruschetta:

4 slices country bread or baguette

olive oil

1 garlic clove (optional)

For the asparagus:

1 pound asparagus spears

To garnish:

a few sautéed mushrooms or wild mushrooms, a few mixed salad leaves, or fresh parsley or chervil sprigs (optional)

Romaine Salad

THIS IS PAUL'S VERSION OF CAESAR SALAD. DONE PROPERLY, WITH FIRST-CLASS INGREDIENTS, IT IS EVERYONE'S FAVORITE SALAD. ALWAYS USE GOOD-QUALITY ANCHOVIES AND OLIVES FOR THE BEST FLAVOR. YOU CAN SAVE A LITTLE TIME BY WHIPPING UP THE DRESSING IN A FOOD PROCESSOR. IT IS WORTH MAKING YOUR OWN GARLIC CROUTONS, AS THEY ARE SO MUCH BETTER THAN STORE-BOUGHT. **Serves 4 to 6** (V)

For the dressing:

1/2 teaspoon salt

1 tablespoon Dijon mustard

4 tablespoons fresh lemon juice

1 garlic clove, crushed

2 tablespoons Worcestershire sauce

10 drops Tabasco sauce

4 anchovy fillets

3/4 cup plus 2 tablespoons light olive oil

For the croutons:

6 slices dense bread

6 tablespoons olive oil

2 garlic cloves

1 large head romaine lettuce

1 cup freshly grated Parmesan cheese

imported black olives

To make the dressing, in a small bowl, dissolve the salt and mustard in the lemon juice. Add the garlic, Worcestershire sauce, and Tabasco sauce. Crush the anchovy fillets through a garlic press, then add them to the bowl. Slowly whisk in the olive oil a drop at a time, gradually incorporating it into the rest of the mixture. Taste and adjust the seasoning.

Preheat the oven to 325 degrees F.

To make croutons, drizzle or brush the bread slices on both sides with the olive oil and toast in the preheated oven for about 10 minutes, or until crisp and golden. Remove them from the oven and while they are still hot, rub the peeled garlic cloves all over both sides, then cut into cubes.

To serve, tear the bigger outer leaves of the lettuce roughly and use the small inside ones whole. Place in a large salad bowl and toss with the dressing and two-thirds of the grated Parmesan. Attractively arrange a big pile in the center of each plate and garnish with as many of the garlic croutons and black olives as you fancy. Top it all off with the remaining Parmesan.

Spiced Pumpkin Pie
with Cinnamon Cream

PUMPKIN HAS A FINE, DELICATE FLAVOR THAT TOO MANY PEOPLE MISS OUT ON BY CARELESS COOKING. BY BAKING THE FLESH IN ITS OWN SHELL, THE NATURAL SWEETNESS IS INTENSIFIED, THE TEXTURE IS UNADULTERATED, AND THE FLAVOR CAN REALLY COME THROUGH. **Serves 8**

Preheat the oven to 350 degrees F. Lightly butter an 8-inch pie dish with sloping sides. To prepare the tart base, on a lightly floured board, roll out the pastry about 1/8 inch thick. Fit the pastry into the prepared pie dish. Chill in the refrigerator for 20 minutes.

Line the pastry-lined dish with parchment paper (or aluminum foil) and fill with pie weights or dried beans. Bake blind in the preheated oven for 12 minutes, or until the base is a light golden brown. Remove from oven, remove the weights or beans and paper, and brush the inside with the egg yolk to seal the pastry. Set aside.

To prepare the pumpkin, cut it in half, scoop out and discard the seeds and stringy bits, and place the pumpkin in a roasting pan, cut side down. Bake in the preheated oven for about 1 hour, or until it is tender and falling apart. Scrape the cooked flesh off the shell and press through a sieve. The sieved flesh should be quite dry. Measure out 1 1/2 cups.

Whisk together the brown sugar, eggs, spices, and salt until well dissolved. Stir in the pumpkin flesh, and cream until smooth. Finally, add the Cognac and taste. Pour the mixture into the prebaked pie shell and cook in the preheated oven for 30 to 35 minutes, or until set. Remove from the oven and leave to cool. It will continue to firm and set as it cools.

To prepare the cinnamon cream, whisk the cream until it holds soft peaks. Add the superfine sugar and cinnamon and whisk again until they have dissolved. The cream should just hold firm peaks. It should be mildly sweet and fragrant with the taste and aroma of cinnamon. Cover and chill until serving.

To serve the pie, cut it into wedges and serve garnished with a generous dollop of the cinnamon cream. This pie tastes best when just slightly warm or at room temperature rather than chilled.

7 ounces Sweet Shortcrust Pastry (see page 184)

1 egg yolk, lightly beaten

1 medium pumpkin

1 cup firmly packed brown sugar

4 eggs, lightly beaten

1 1/2 teaspoons ground cinnamon

1/2 teaspoon freshly grated nutmeg

1 teaspoon ground ginger

1/4 teaspoon ground cloves

1 tablespoon freshly grated ginger root

1/4 teaspoon salt

3/4 cup whipping cream

3 tablespoons Cognac or other Brandy

For the cinnamon cream:

1 cup whipping cream

2/3 cup superfine caster sugar

1 tablespoon ground cinnamon

Carrot Cake

ALMOST EVERY HOUSEHOLD HAS ITS OWN VERSION OF CARROT CAKE WITH SLIGHTLY VARYING INGREDIENTS, FROM PINEAPPLE TO RAISINS. THE IMPORTANT THING HERE IS THAT THE CARROT GIVES THE CAKE MOISTURE, SWEETNESS, AND A TERRIFIC KEEPING QUALITY. FRESH, TASTY CARROTS ENSURE THE BEST RESULTS. **Serves 10 to 12** (V)

1 cup plus 2 tablespoons (9 ounces) unsalted butter, at room temperature

2 cups superfine sugar

grated zest of 2 oranges

4 eggs

1 pound carrots, peeled and grated

rounded 1 cup almonds or pecans, chopped

1 tablespoon vanilla extract

2 cups all-purpose flour

2 teaspoons baking soda

1 teaspoon mixed spices such as pumpkin pie spice

1 teaspoon salt

For the icing:

8 ounces cream cheese, at room temperature

5 tablespoons unsalted butter, at room temperature

3 1/2 cup confectioners' sugar, sifted

1 teaspoon vanilla extract

Preheat the oven to 350 degrees F. Butter a 9-inch springform pan.

In a bowl, beat together the butter, superfine sugar, and orange zest until light and fluffy. Add the eggs one at a time, beating well to incorporate each addition fully before adding more. Fold in the carrots and nuts. Add the vanilla extract. Finally, sift together the flour, baking soda, spices, and salt into a bowl. Fold into the cake mixture. Pour the mixture into the prepared springform pan.

Bake in the preheated oven for 45 to 60 minutes. The sides of the cake should be coming away from the sides of the pan and a skewer inserted into the center of the cake should come out clean.

To make the icing, beat the cream cheese and butter together until smooth. Add the confectioners' sugar and vanilla extract and again beat until smooth. This frosting is rich, thick, and delicious. Spread the icing generously over the top of the cake.

CHAPTER THIRTEEN

The Potato Field

The potato was introduced to Ireland in the 1700s. Less than one hundred years later, nearly all laborers and their families were dependent on it for subsistence. The disaster brought on by a blight that destroyed the entire crop in 1845 is well known. The Great Famine is now only a part of Ireland's history, and the potato is a source of pride and importance to most Irish. Pride, because Ireland is one of the last few places still bothering to grow varieties long lost on the British mainland to those two "virtues," yield and profit. Importance, because the Irish truly love their potatoes; most would admit to eating them at least once a day.

A potato is not just a potato. This was something that Jeanne, having grown up on the Canadian prairies, never really understood until she moved to Ireland. What makes a good baking potato compared to a good salad potato? Which is best for frying and which is good for mashing? Several years later, she's not only appreciating the difference, she's demanding it! Floury potatoes, such as russet or Idaho, are good for deep-frying, baking, and mashing. Salads require a firmer, more waxy potato like any of the red-skinned varieties. New potatoes are those that are harvested when still immature; they tend to have crisp, tender flesh. Selecting potatoes isn't easy, but it is worth the effort. Two of the best known Irish potato dishes are champ (also known as stelk) made with scallions, and Colcannon made with cabbage.

Another traditional method of cooking potatoes is to simply boil them in their jackets. This not only holds the potatoes in shape, but it keeps in the nutrition as well. The potato must also be one of the most popular soup vegetables, adding texture, substance, and flavor.

Storing potatoes properly also takes a bit of care and thought. Be sure to remove them from those plastic bags in which the supermarket sells them. Keep them in a cool, dry, and dark place. Best of all, get out to the country to buy direct from a farmer if you can.

Champp

WE LIKE TO EAT CHAMP AS A DISH ON ITS OWN, WHICH IS REALLY THE PROPER WAY. FOR US, IT IS THE ULTIMATE COMFORT FOOD, REMINDING US OF CHILDHOOD, SCHOOL LUNCHES, AND MUM. **Serves 4** Ⓥ

Peel and quarter the potatoes. Place them in a large pan, cover with salted water, and bring to a boil. Reduce the heat and simmer for 20 to 30 minutes, or until the potatoes are just cooked. Pour off the water, cover the pan, and let it stand for about 3 minutes; this allows the potatoes to become soft and completely cooked.

While the potatoes are resting, finely chop the scallions. Combine the milk and butter in a small pan and bring to a boil. Put the chopped onions into the boiling mixture, then remove from the heat and let them infuse for 1 minute. This mellows out the raw onion taste. Mash the potatoes, then stir in the milk mixture until the whole mixture is smooth. Check seasoning and add salt if necessary. Serve on its own in warmed bowls with a spoonful of butter on top.

2 1/4 pounds floury potatoes

6 large scallions

1 1/4 cups milk

4 tablespoons unsalted butter

salt

unsalted butter for serving

Colcannon

COLCANNON IS TO THE SOUTH OF IRELAND WHAT CHAMP IS TO THE NORTH, A COMFORT FOOD, A WARM, SATISFYING, HOMELY DISH. THIS IS EUGENE O'CALLAGHAN'S—OF EUGENE'S RESTAURANT IN COUNTY WEXFORD—OLD FAMILY RECIPE. **Serves 6** Ⓥ

Line the bottom of a deep, heavy-bottomed saucepan with a layer of the quartered potatoes. On top of this, place a layer of onions, then a layer of sliced cabbage, then a layer of parsnips. Repeat the layering until all the ingredients are used up. Measure out the water, add the salt to it, and pour it into the saucepan. Top it all off with the cabbage leaves. Cover with a lid and gently bring to a boil. Cook gently for about 1 hour.

Remove the cabbage leaves from the top, and roughly mash all the cooked vegetables together. Serve with lots of butter and freshly chopped parsley.

1 1/2 pounds floury potatoes, peeled and quartered

2 or 3 medium onions (11 ounces), finely chopped

1/2 head white cabbage, cored and thinly sliced

2 large parsnips, peeled and cut into wedges

1 1/4 cups water

1 teaspoon salt

3 large cabbage leaves

unsalted butter for serving

chopped fresh parsley

Potato Torte
with Cabbage, Bacon, and Cheddar

THIS TASTY TORTE CAN BE A LUNCHEON DISH IN ITS OWN RIGHT, SERVED WITH A GREEN SALAD, OR OFFERED AS AN ACCOMPANIMENT. **Serves 8** Ⓥ

4 1/2 cups water

1/2 head Savoy cabbage, outer leaves discarded, cored, and thinly sliced

7 ounces bacon, cut into 1/2-inch pieces

2 tablespoons unsalted butter

1 1/2 cups floury potatoes

salt and freshly ground black pepper

7 ounces Cheddar cheese, grated

Preheat the oven to 400 degrees F.

In a saucepan, bring the water to a boil, add the cabbage, and cook for 2 minutes. Drain, refresh in cold water, dry thoroughly, and place in a bowl.

In a frying pan, sauté the bacon in the butter over medium heat until it is just starting to brown. Using a slotted spoon, remove the bacon from the fat. Reserve the fat, and toss the bacon with the cabbage.

Peel and slice the potatoes 1/8 inch thick. Rinse and dry the potato slices and season them lightly with salt and pepper. Then toss them in the bacon fat.

In a large nonstick pan or baking dish, arrange a layer of potatoes on the bottom. Sprinkle lightly with some of the cheese. Top with a layer of cabbage and bacon, and again sprinkle lightly with cheese. Continue building the torte in this fashion until all the ingredients are used up. It is important that each layer is sprinkled with cheese, as this helps to hold the torte together.

Cover the pan with a circle of parchment paper, and bake in the oven for 45 minutes. Remove from the oven and allow to cool to room temperature. Remove the parchment paper, and turn the torte out onto a cutting board.

To serve, carefully cut into portions with a sharp knife.

Warm Potato Pancake
with Smoked Salmon and Chive Crème Fraîche

THIS POTATO PANCAKE RECIPE IS VERY VERSATILE. ADD SOME CORN KERNELS, SAUTÉED LEEKS, OR FRESH TRUFFLE TO THE BATTER, IF YOU LIKE. IT CAN BE SERVED AS AN ACCOMPANIMENT TO A MAIN COURSE OR SIMPLY ON ITS OWN WITH BUTTER. **Serves 8**

Preheat the oven to 350 degrees F.

Prepare the smoked salmon by trimming off any dark pieces. Carefully roll up each slice so that it makes a neat bundle or rosette.

Place the potatoes in a pan, add salted water to cover, and bring to a boil. Reduce the heat to simmer and cook for 20 to 30 minutes, or until tender. Drain well and mash the potatoes, making sure there are no lumps. Gently stir in the flour and then the egg yolks. Beat in just enough of the cream, a spoonful at a time, to form a thick batter the consistency of a medium porridge. Do not add all 4 tablespoons of the cream if the batter is thin enough. This will depend on the amount of water the potatoes absorbed during cooking. In a separate bowl, whisk the egg whites until they are light and frothy, then fold into the batter.

Heat a small ovenproof frying pan over gentle heat until it is very hot. Add the butter, let it foam, and add a large spoonful or two of the batter. It will spread a little and find its own thickness. Cook for 3 to 4 minutes over a gentle heat until the entire pancake seems to be setting. Turn it over and cook for a further 2 minutes. Place it in the warmed oven, still in the frying pan, for 1 to 2 minutes; this will help to set the entire pancake. This is not absolutely necessary, but it will help to ensure that it is properly cooked. Drain briefly on paper towels and continue to cook the rest of the pancakes in the same manner.

To make the chive crème fraîche, mix the crème fraîche with the chives, a few drops of lemon juice, and some salt and pepper to taste.

To serve, place a pancake on each plate. Top with a rosette of smoked salmon and a large dollop of the crème fraîche.

6 large slices smoked salmon, about 2 ounces each

8 to 9 ounces floury potatoes, peeled and quartered

2 tablespoons all-purpose flour

2 eggs, separated

4 tablespoons whipping cream

2 tablespoons unsalted butter

For the chive crème fraîche:

1 cup crème fraîche

1 bunch fresh chives, finely snipped

1/2 lemon

salt and freshly ground white pepper

Ulster Fry

WHAT MAKES AN ULSTER FRY DIFFERENT OR BETTER THAN ANY OTHER FRY? IT'S THE FRIED SODA AND POTATO BREADS, OF COURSE. IF THIS WASN'T SUCH A CHOLESTEROL-PACKED DISH, PAUL COULD EAT IT EVERY DAY! **Serves 4**

2 slices bacon heavily streaked with fat

2 tablespoons vegetable oil

4 slices lean bacon

1 ripe tomato, halved

salt and freshly ground white pepper

1 Irish Soda Farl (see page 152)

2 Potato Bread scones (see page 143)

1 teaspoon unsalted butter

4 free-range eggs

2 tablespoons water

Fry the streaky bacon in a large frying pan with the vegetable oil. When almost cooked, add the lean bacon and the tomato halves, and season the tomatoes with salt and pepper. Cook until the streaky slices are crispy, the lean bacon is cooked but not dried out, and the tomatoes are just beginning to soften. Transfer them all to a warm oven, reserving the fat in the pan.

Cut the soda bread farl in half lengthwise and then each side in half again, ending up with 4 pieces. Cut the potato bread scones in two. Dip the pieces into the fat that was left in the pan, let them soak up a little, and then drain away any excess. Dry-fry the pieces of bread gently in the same pan until they are starting to crisp up. Remove them from the pan and reserve in a warm oven.

To fry the eggs allow the butter to melt in a nonstick pan until it is sizzling. Crack the eggs carefully into the pan, add the water and a little salt, and cover the pan. Allow them to cook slowly for about 2 minutes, or until they are done to your taste.

Serve at once on warm plates, dividing up the bacon, bread, tomato, and eggs evenly.

Potato Bread

THIS SIMPLE GRIDDLE BREAD IS SO MOIST AND FLAVORSOME THAT IT DOESN'T REALLY NEED THE REST OF THE ULSTER FRY. THIS IS PAUL'S MOTHER'S VERSION. **Serves 4** (V)

1 1/2 pounds floury potatoes, freshly boiled and still hot

1/2 cup all-purpose flour

a pinch of salt

2 to 4 tablespoons unsalted butter, melted

Preheat a griddle or heavy frying pan until hot. Peel the potatoes and place in a bowl. Mash until very smooth. While the potatoes are still hot, sprinkle on the flour and salt and mix together. Add as much of the melted butter as is needed to give the dough a workable feel and knead briefly; do not knead too much or the dough will toughen.

On a floured work surface, roll out the dough into a big circle about 1/2 inch thick. Cut into quarters and cook on the hot griddle until brown. This will take about 3 minutes. Turn over and cook on the other side for about 2 minutes.

These potato breads are best eaten fresh, but they will keep quite well and can be reheated the following day.

Creamy Potato Gratin

JEANNE'S SISTER-IN-LAW SAYS THAT SHE SHOULD GIVE UP COOKING ALL OTHER POTATO RECIPES AND JUST USE THIS ONE. **Serves 4** (V)

1 pound floury potatoes, peeled and thinly sliced

salt and freshly ground white pepper

a pinch of freshly grated nutmeg

1 garlic clove, finely chopped

5 cups whipping cream

Preheat the oven to 325 degrees F. Put the sliced potatoes into a large bowl and season with salt and pepper and a pinch of nutmeg. Rub the seasonings into the potatoes with your hands to ensure that they are evenly distributed. Mix the garlic with the cream, and then mix well with the rest of the ingredients in the bowl.

Tip the mixture into a heavy ceramic gratin dish and pat down the slices. Cover with parchment paper or aluminum foil. Cook in the preheated oven for 1 hour, or until the potatoes are tender when pierced.

If desired, you can remove the paper or foil and brown the top under a hot broiler for about 2 minutes, or until golden brown.

Two Ways with New Potatoes

PAUL GREW UP IN COUNTY DOWN, WHICH IS FAMOUS FOR ITS COMBER POTATOES. EACH YEAR WE ARE AMAZED BY THE DELICACY OF NEW POTATOES. WHEN FRESHLY DUG, THEIR FINE SKIN CAN BE EASED OFF WITH THUMB AND FOREFINGER, AND THE FLAVOR IS SWEET AND PURE. AFTER A DAY THE SKIN STARTS TO TOUGHEN, AND IT SEEMS TO PAUL THAT THEY LOSE A LITTLE OF THEIR FINESSE. SO TREAT NEW POTATOES AS YOU WOULD ANY DELICATE VEGETABLE, BUYING THEM AS CLOSE TO THE SOURCE AND AS FRESH AS POSSIBLE.

General Preparation: Wash and lightly scrub the potatoes in cold water. Place in a large saucepan, add water to cover, and 1 tablespoon salt. Bring to a boil, and then reduce the heat and simmer for 10 to 15 minutes, or until the tip of a knife pierces each potato easily. Drain and cover until ready to use.

New Potatoes with Creamed Horseradish and Smoked Salmon

Serves 4 as a starter

9 ounces new potatoes, freshly boiled and sliced while still hot

salt and freshly ground white pepper

1 tablespoon finely snipped fresh chives

1 tablespoon roughly chopped fresh dill

2 tablespoons prepared horseradish

smoked salmon, cut into julienne strips

Place the potato slices in a bowl and lightly season with some salt and pepper. Toss gently with the chives, dill, and horseradish while still warm. Top with strips of smoked salmon and serve.

New Potatoes with Peas and Ham

Serves 4 Ⓥ

1 cup shelled peas

4 tablespoons water

pinch of salt

4 tablespoons unsalted butter

3 ounces cooked ham, cut into 1/4-inch dice

9 ounces new potatoes, freshly boiled and still hot

1 tablespoon chopped fresh mint or parsley

Put the peas, water, salt, and 1 tablespoon of the butter into a medium saucepan. Cover and cook vigorously for 3 minutes, or until the peas are just cooked. Add the ham, potatoes, mint or parsley, and the remaining 3 tablespoons butter. Shake the pan gently until the butter becomes creamy and saucelike. Serve at once. This is an ideal accompaniment to spring lamb.

Baked Potato Skins
with Avocado, Cheddar, and Salsa

AN AGELESS SNACK, GREAT FOR WATCHING SPORTS ON TV, FOR SITTING AROUND A FIRE, FOR AN "AFTER-THE-PUB" NIBBLE, OR EVEN FOR A COCKTAIL PARTY. KIDS LOVE IT, TOO! **Serves 4** (v)

Preheat the oven to 325 degrees F. Bake the potatoes in the preheated oven for 1 hour. (Or you can cook them in a microwave oven on High for about 20 minutes.)

When they are cooked, cut each potato in half lengthwise and scoop out most of the potato pulp to form boatlike shapes. Reserve the scooped out portion for another use. Cut each half in half again so that you have 4 lengthwise quarters. Raise the oven temperature to 400 degrees F.

Preheat the vegetable oil in a deep-fat fryer or deep pan to 350 degrees F, or until a cube of bread turns golden within 1 minute. Working in batches, deep-fry the skins for about 4 minutes, or until nice and crisp. Transfer the skins to paper towels to drain, then season with salt.

Arrange the skins open side up on a baking sheet. Top with the diced avocado, scallions, and cheese. Bake in the preheated oven for 5 minutes, or until the cheese is nicely melted and beginning to brown.

To serve, top with spoonfuls of salsa and sprinkle with pepper and lots of cilantro.

6 large baking potatoes

9 cups vegetable oil

salt

2 avocados, pitted, peeled, and diced

4 scallions, thinly sliced

9 ounces Cheddar cheese, grated

Mexican-style salsa

freshly ground black pepper

1 bunch fresh cilantro, chopped

The Watermill

Watermills have been a part of the Irish landscape since medieval times. The abundant source of water that her climate guarantees accounts for a large number of fast-flowing streams throughout the countryside, and to harness this energy was only logical. It wasn't until the end of the nineteenth century, with the introduction of the steam engine, that the reliance on these mills for food production (and industrial use as well) went into slow decline.

Oats were probably the most common grain in days gone by, but barley, rye, and wheat were also grown and milled. Today, there are relatively few mills actually in production. Those that are seem to be aimed mostly at the health, or alternative, food market, producing organic wheat and its products. Hopefully, however, as more people raise their standards through growing knowledge about what they are eating, these types of wholesome food producers will be more in demand. Congratulations to those determined enough to be pioneers of the movement toward better quality food products.

What can be as satisfying and nourishing as a wholesome loaf of bread? In some form or another, it has been the mainstay of Western man's diet for centuries. This holds true in Ireland as well. Having said that, however, the staple breads of this island have two variations that set them apart. First, it was only in the last few decades that yeast has been widespread as a leavening agent. Traditionally, buttermilk and, later, baking soda were used. Second, the traditional Irish hearth had no oven, consequently all the breads were either cooked on a griddle set above the fire or in a type of enclosed pot or Dutch oven that could be set among the coals. As a result, Ireland boasts a wealth of various soda breads, scones, griddle cakes, and the like, all of which can quite easily be reproduced in a heavy frying pan on the top of a modern stove. Don't be afraid of them. It's simply another technique for you to master.

One area every Irish kitchen seems to get a high rating in is baking. Making cakes, biscuits, and tea breads was and is a tradition in which the Irish housewife tends to pride herself. Nowadays, with home baking seeming to be in decline for the most part elsewhere, it's absolutely delightful to walk into a home and smell those enticing aromas. Paul's mother and aunt are great examples of this lingering tradition. We have learned so much over the years from them both. It is just a shame that everyone can't have a grandma, aunt, or mother to pass on all these precious, gratifying secrets.

Crusty Farmhouse White Bread

THERE'S NOTHING LIKE THE HEADY AROMA OF BREAD, FRESH FROM THE OVEN. IT IS A BALANCED HARMONY OF SIMPLE INGREDIENTS AND IT TRULY IS WORTH EVERY SHRED OF EFFORT IT IS GIVEN. YOU CAN BAKE THE LOAVES IN PANS OR SHAPE THEM HOWEVER YOU CHOOSE. **Makes two 1-pound loaves** Ⓥ

scant 2 tablespoons active dry yeast (2 packages) or 1 ounce fresh yeast

3 3/4 cups warm water (about 104 degrees F)

7 cups bread flour

2 tablespoons salt

4 tablespoons unsalted butter

Combine the yeast with one-third of the warm water and leave for 10 minutes until it becomes frothy and foamy. (This is called "proofing the yeast.")

Put the flour, salt, and butter into a stand mixer fitted with a dough hook. Process on medium speed, adding all the yeast liquid and the remaining water together. Beat on medium speed until the dough has come together, looks rather shiny, and has a nice elasticity. It should not be sticky. Alternatively, stir together the ingredients and then knead by hand. This will take considerably longer.

Turn out the dough into a large, clean, oiled bowl and cover with oiled plastic wrap. Leave to rise at room temperature for 1 1/2 to 2 hours, or until it has doubled in size.

If you prefer a more developed flavor and have the time, punch down the dough, again form into a ball, and return the dough to the bowl to rise a second time. This time need not be quite so long; 1 to 1 1/2 hours should suffice.

Oil 2 standard loaf pans or 2 baking sheets. To form the loaves to be baked in the bread pans, you don't really have to punch down the dough. The shaping of the loaf will usually dispel the bubbles enough and reactivate the gluten and yeast. First, divide the dough in half. Flatten the first piece using the heel of your hand, then fold the dough over on itself. Basically, you are rolling a long cylinder shape. Roll it back and forth a little to smooth the surface. When it is placed into the pan, the fold should be at the bottom. Repeat with the other piece. Cover the pans with oiled plastic wrap and leave to rise again until doubled in size.

If you are forming round or oval loaves to be baked on a flat baking sheet, you may want to punch down the dough a little more. Simply lift and slap the dough down a few times on your work surface, folding it over on itself in between. With your hands, working the dough in a counterclockwise rotary action, roll one-half of the dough until the folds are tucked underneath and the whole surface is smooth and taut. Place on the prepared baking sheet. Repeat with the other half. Cover the loaves with oiled plastic wrap and leave to rise until doubled in size.

Preheat the oven to 400 degrees F. Just before putting the loaves into the preheated oven, slash the surface firmly with a very sharp knife. Besides being decorative, this makes for more crust, which appeals to some individuals. Spray the loaves generously with a mister at this point as well; this improves the crust by making it more crisp.

Bake in the preheated oven for 15 minutes, then reduce the oven temperature to 350 degrees F for a further 30 minutes to ensure that the crust does not brown too much. The loaves are cooked when you tap the bottom and get a good hollow sound. Cool on a wire rack and do not wrap until completely cool.

OVERLEAF:

Left: Pear and Chocolate Almond Cream Tart with Chocolate Sauce (page 154)

Center: Decadent Chocolate Brownies (page 159)

Right: Oatmeal Muffins (page 153)

Background: Crusty Farmhouse White Bread (page 148)

Wheaten Bread

FOR THOSE WHO HAVE NEITHER THE TIME NOR THE INCLINATION TO MAKE THE PRECEDING YEAST BREAD, THIS LOAF IS SIMPLICITY ITSELF. THROW THE INGREDIENTS TOGETHER, BAKE IT OFF, AND VOILÀ—A VERY QUICK, HASSLE-FREE, AND TASTY LOAF. **Makes one 2-pound loaf** Ⓥ

Preheat the oven to 400 degrees F. Generously grease a large loaf pan.

In a large bowl, stir all the dry ingredients together. Stir in the buttermilk to form a thick batter. Pour into the prepared pan.

Bake in the preheated oven for 1 to 1 1/2 hours, or until nicely browned. The loaf is cooked when you tap the bottom and get a hollow sound. Cool on a wire rack. Alternatively, if you prefer a softer crust, wrap in a lightly dampened cloth and leave to cool.

2 1/2 cups whole-wheat flour, preferably a coarse one

1 cup all-purpose flour

4 tablespoons wheat bran

2 teaspoons baking soda

1/2 teaspoon salt

1 tablespoon brown sugar

1 3/4 to 2 cups buttermilk

1 teaspoon cream of tartar

Irish Soda Farls

THESE GRIDDLE BREADS KEEP BETTER THAN OVEN-BAKED SODA BREAD. SPLIT IN TWO AND SERVED WITH PLENTY OF BUTTER AND JAM, THEY ARE THE PERFECT MATCH FOR A MORNING CUP OF TEA. **Serves 4** ⓥ

3 1/4 cups all-purpose flour

3/4 teaspoon baking soda

a pinch of salt

a pinch of sugar

1 teaspoon vegetable oil

scant 2 cups to 2 1/4 cups buttermilk

unsalted butter for serving

Preheat a griddle or heavy frying pan to hot but not smoking. Sift together the flour, baking soda, salt, and sugar into a bowl and make a well in the center. Pour in the oil and the lesser quantity of buttermilk and mix gently and quickly together. The resulting dough should be soft and fairly slack; add more buttermilk if necessary.

Turn out onto a work surface and knead lightly for 1 minute. Work into a large flat cake 1/2 inch to 3/4 inch thick. If it is any thicker, it may not cook through properly. Cut a deep cross through the surface to make 4 farls (triangular cakes).

The griddle or pan should be hot enough to brown a little flour when it is sprinkled on it; the heat should be somewhere between medium to hot. Place the farls onto the griddle and cook for 6 to 10 minutes on each side. If the crust starts to burn, the griddle or pan is too hot.

To serve, split each farl in half horizontally and spread thickly with butter. When a day or two old, the farls can be split and toasted and will be equally delicious.

Oatmeal Muffins

FOR THOSE WHO CANNOT FACE UP TO A STEAMING BOWL OF PORRIDGE EVERY MORNING, THESE MUFFINS OFFER A QUICK, EASY, AND JUST AS HEALTHY ALTERNATIVE. THEY COULD BE MADE SWEETER, IF DESIRED, BUT WHEN MADE AS FOLLOWS, THERE IS A WHOLESOME, NUTRITIOUS FEELING TO THEM. USE GOOD, OLD-FASHIONED OATS, NOT THE INSTANT VARIETIES. THESE MUFFINS COULD BE FILLED WITH ANY VARIETY OF FRUIT, DRIED FRUIT, OR FLAVORING. JUST REMEMBER TO BE GENEROUS WITH WHATEVER YOU CHOOSE. THE MOST IMPORTANT FACTOR FOR GREAT MUFFINS IS TO AVOID OVERMIXING, WHICH WOULD RESULT IN A TOUGH, CHEWY MUFFIN. **Makes 24 muffins** (V)

In a bowl, leave the oats to soak in the buttermilk in the refrigerator overnight or for at least a few hours. Preheat the oven to 350 degrees F. Line 24 standard muffin cups with paper liners.

Sift together the flour, baking soda, and salt into a large bowl. Combine the brown sugar and lemon zest and add it to the bowl. Stir to combine, then stir in the oats mixture. Stir in the melted butter and eggs until just combined. Finally, fold in the dates and apple. Note that the apple must be chopped quite finely to ensure that it cooks completely in the short cooking time. Spoon the batter into the paper liners, filling them two-thirds full.

Bake in the preheated oven for 17 to 20 minutes. Muffin tins vary in the size of their molds, so baking time can vary as well. Cool on wire racks and eat immediately, or keep in an airtight container if desired.

2 2/3 cups rolled oats

3 cups buttermilk

2 1/4 cups all-purpose flour

1 1/2 teaspoons baking soda

1/2 teaspoon salt

1 cup firmly packed brown sugar

grated zest of 1 lemon

3 tablespoons unsalted butter, melted and cooled

3 eggs

2/3 cup dates, chopped and tossed in just enough flour to coat

1 cup peeled and finely chopped apple, tossed in the juice of 1 lemon

Pear and Chocolate Almond Cream Tart
with Chocolate Sauce

PEARS AND CHOCOLATE GO TOGETHER BEAUTIFULLY. THIS ALMOND CREAM CAN BE MADE WITHOUT

CHOCOLATE; IT THEN MARRIES WELL WITH APRICOTS, PEACHES, OR CHERRIES. **Serves 8** Ⓥ

For the tart:

9 ounces Sweet Shortcrust Pastry (see page 184)

1 egg yolk, lightly beaten

1/2 recipe Chocolate Almond Cream (see page 185), removed from the refrigerator to soften

4 to 6 poached pears (see page 187), drained, halved, cored, and sliced into fans

4 to 5 tablespoons sliced or chopped blanched almonds

For the glaze:

3 tablespoons apricot jam

3 tablespoons Sugar Syrup (see page 188) or poaching liquid from pears

For the chocolate sauce:

12 ounces semisweet chocolate

1 1/4 cups milk or light cream, or half milk and half light cream

1/3 cup superfine sugar

4 tablespoons unsalted butter

Butter a 9- or 10-inch fluted tart pan with a removable bottom.

To make the tart, on a lightly flour board, roll out the pastry about 1/4 inch thick. Fit into the prepared pan and trim the edges even. Leave to rest in the refrigerator for at least 30 minutes.

Preheat the oven to 350 degrees F. Line the pastry-lined pan with parchment paper (or aluminum foil) and fill with pie weights or dried beans. Bake blind in the preheated oven for about 10 minutes, or until golden. Remove the weights and paper. Brush the inside lightly with the egg yolk. This helps to seal the pastry during cooking.

Reduce the oven temperature to 325 degrees F.

Using a pastry bag or a palette knife, evenly distribute the almond cream over the base of the tart; it should be no more than 3/4 inch thick. Arrange the pear fans decoratively on top of the almond cream, pressing them gently into the cream. Sprinkle the almonds generously over the top, and place the tart on a baking sheet.

Bake in the preheated oven for 30 to 45 minutes. It is important that the almond cream be completely cooked. A skewer inserted into the middle should come out clean. Remove from the oven and let cool on a wire rack.

A light glaze will improve the tart's appearance. To do this, melt a few tablespoons of apricot jam with an equal amount of Sugar Syrup or poaching liquid from the pears. When it has come to a boil, use a pastry brush to coat the top of the tart lightly. The shiny appearance will not interfere with the flavor of the tart.

To make the sauce, melt the chocolate very gently in the top pan of a double boiler over gently simmering water or in a heatproof bowl placed over a saucepan of simmering water. Set aside. Place the milk and/or cream, superfine sugar, and butter in a saucepan and bring to a boil, stirring to dissolve the sugar. Remove from the heat and let cool until warm. (If added to the chocolate while still hot, this mixture would scald the chocolate and impart a burnt, acrid flavor to the sauce.) Whisk the chocolate into the milk mixture until smooth and well combined. (This sauce keeps very well in the refrigerator and just needs to be taken out and warmed gently when needed.)

Serve wedges of tart with the warm chocolate sauce.

Poached Pears
with Lime Sabayon

A SIMPLE YET PLEASING DESSERT. BE VERY GENEROUS WITH THE SABAYON, AS EVERYONE LOVES IT.

Serves 4 (V)

Halve and core each pear. With a sharp knife, slice each half in a fan style and lay them in a shallow dish. Add just enough of the poaching syrup to cover, lace well with 3 to 4 tablespoons of the lime juice, and leave to macerate for 1 to 2 hours.

To make the sabayon, place the egg yolks, the superfine sugar, and the salt into a stainless-steel bowl. Whisk together gently. Add the dessert wine or Champagne and the remaining poaching syrup. Whisk vigorously over (not touching) barely simmering water until thick and pale, for about 10 minutes. It should leave traces in the bottom of the bowl, and also leave a good, thick ribbon when dropped back on itself. Whisk in enough lime juice to impart a firm tartness.

To serve, place the pear halves in a yin-yang fashion on slightly warmed plates, and spoon the sabayon generously over them. Garnish with a mint sprig or candied lime julienne.

4 poached pears (see page 187)

generous 1/2 cup poaching syrup from the pears

6 to 8 tablespoons fresh lime juice

6 egg yolks

scant 2/3 cup superfine sugar

pinch of salt

1/2 cup plus 1 1/2 teaspoons dessert wine or Champagne

fresh mint sprigs or candied lime julienne

Fruit Loaf Bread and Butter Pudding

INFUSING THE CUSTARD BASE WITH FRESH ORANGE BRINGS OUT THE FRUIT FLAVORS IN THIS LOAF. WE FIND THIS INTERPRETATION FAR MORE INTERESTING THAN THE USUAL ONE. MAKING THE LOAF IN A MIXER OR FOOD PROCESSOR IS QUICKER AND MUCH EASIER THAN BY HAND. **Serves 8** (v)

For the loaf:

scant 1 tablespoon active dry yeast (1 package) or 1/2 ounce fresh yeast

3 tablespoons warm milk

2 3/4 cups all-purpose flour

1 teaspoon salt

2 tablespoons sugar

4 eggs

1 cup (8 ounces) plus 6 tablespoons unsalted butter, at room temperature

3 tablespoons finely chopped glacé cherries

3 tablespoons finely chopped candied citrus peel

1/3 cup dark or golden raisins

For the pudding:

2 cups plus 2 tablespoons milk

2 cups plus 2 tablespoons whipping cream

1 teaspoon vanilla extract

1/2 orange

1 cup plus 2 tablespoons sugar

4 whole eggs

6 egg yolks

Butter a standard loaf pan. Dissolve the yeast in the warm milk and leave in a warm place for about 10 minutes until foamy and frothy. Place the flour, salt, sugar, and eggs in the bowl of a stand mixer or in a mixing bowl. Add the yeast mixture and mix with a dough hook on medium speed for about 3 minutes, or by hand with a wooden spoon, until the dough comes together. Slowly, little by little, add the butter, fully incorporating each addition before adding more. The dough should turn shiny, elastic, and be quite soft. Finally, toss in the candied fruits and raisins. Turn into a greased bowl and cover with oiled plastic wrap. Leave to rise in a warm place for about 1 hour, or until doubled in size.

Turn the dough out onto a work surface and shape to fit into the prepared loaf pan. Cover with oiled plastic wrap and leave to rise again until doubled in size. This time it should not take as long, about 40 minutes.

Preheat the oven to 375 degrees F. Bake the loaf in the center of the preheated oven for about 45 minutes, or until nicely browned. It should sound hollow when tapped on the bottom. Leave to cool on a wire rack. (This loaf will freeze very well if wrapped tightly in plastic wrap.)

To make the pudding, put the milk, cream, vanilla extract, and orange in a pan over medium heat and bring to a boil. Set aside and leave to infuse for about 20 minutes.

Preheat the oven to 300 degrees F. In a bowl, whisk together the sugar, whole eggs, and egg yolks until the sugar has dissolved and the mixture is light and fluffy. Strain in the hot cream mixture, whisking continuously. Strain again through a fine-mesh sieve. Set aside.

Cut 8 slices each 1/4-inch thick from the loaf. Cut off the crusts and dry out the slices either in the oven or by toasting them lightly in a toaster.

Arrange the slices attractively in 8 ovenproof bowls and gently pour in the pudding mixture until the bowls are nearly full. Place the bowls in a roasting pan and pour hot water into the pan to reach one-third of the way up the sides of the bowls. Cover with plastic wrap. (Don't worry that the cling film will melt; the oven is not hot enough. The cling film will prevent a crust from forming on the pudding and it will also help to distribute the heat more evenly.)

Bake in the preheated oven for about 30 minutes, or until the puddings are just set; the centers will still be wobbly. Remove from the oven and discard the plastic wrap. Leave the bowls to cool in the water. Some people prefer their pudding still warm, while others prefer it slightly chilled. Serve it however you prefer.

Gypsy Creams

THIS IS ANOTHER ONE OF THOSE TREASURED RECIPES HANDED ON TO JEANNE FROM PAUL'S MUM AND AUNT, FROM THEIR MUM, AND SO ON. A PERFECT ACCOMPANIMENT TO AFTERNOON TEA. **Makes about 2 dozen** (V)

Preheat the oven to 325 degrees F. Using an electric mixer, beat together the butter, shortening, and the sugar until light and fluffy. Meanwhile, mix the boiling water with the golden syrup. Pour this into the butter mixture and beat together. Sift together the baking soda and self-rising flour into a bowl, and fold into the butter mixture. Then fold in the oats until fully incorporated.

On a lightly floured surface, roll out the dough about 1/2 inch thick. Using a cutter 1 1/4 to 1 1/2 inches in diameter, cut out rounds. Place the rounds on an ungreased baking sheet.

Bake for about 12 minutes in the preheated oven, or until golden brown. Let cool on wire racks.

To make the icing, beat together the butter and confectioners' sugar until light and fluffy. Add the coffee extract. The icing should be neither too runny, nor too thick. It should be a spreadable consistency, similar to the texture of peanut butter. When the cookies are cool, sandwich two of them together with a layer of icing spread between them. We like to garnish the tops with a little blob of the icing and a piece of lightly toasted walnut.

1/2 cup (4 ounces) plus 1 tablespoon unsalted butter

1/2 cup (4 ounces) plus 1 tablespoon vegetable shortening

scant 2/3 cup superfine sugar

5 teaspoons boiling water

2 teaspoons golden syrup

2 teaspoons baking soda

2 cups self-rising flour

2 cups rolled oats

For the icing:

1/2 cup (4 ounces) plus 1 tablespoon unsalted butter

2 1/4 cups confectioners' sugar, sifted

a drop or two of coffee extract (or instant coffee dissolved in a few drops of water)

25 walnuts, lightly toasted

Oatmeal and Pecan Cookies

THESE TASTY, CHEWY COOKIES CAN ACCOMPANY COFFEE OR TEA OR GARNISH ICE CREAM.

Makes 24 to 36 (V)

1 cup (8 ounces) unsalted butter, at room temperature

3/4 cup superfine sugar

3/4 cup firmly packed brown sugar

2 eggs

4 tablespoons milk

1 1/2 teaspoons vanilla extract

1 3/4 cups all-purpose flour

1 teaspoon baking soda

1/2 teaspoon salt

1 teaspoon baking powder

2 cups pecans, chopped

1 1/2 cups rolled oats

Using an electric mixer, beat together the butter and the sugars until light and fluffy. In another bowl, mix together the eggs, milk, and vanilla extract. Then, as if making mayonnaise, slowly add the egg mixture to the butter mixture a spoonful at a time, incorporating the liquid into the butter mixture each time before adding more.

Sift together the flour, baking soda, salt, and baking powder. Fold into the egg-butter mixture. Finally, fold in the pecans and oats. Either drop spoon-sized portions onto the ungreased baking sheet, or first roll the spoonfuls into balls and then place them on the sheet. (An ungreased baking sheet should be used, otherwise the cookies will spread too much.) Chill the spoonfuls, or balls, for at least 30 minutes before baking. This allows the butter in the mixture to firm up, again to prevent over-spreading during baking. They will flatten out as they cook and produce a more consistent shape and size of cookie. Preheat the oven to 350 degrees F.

Bake in the preheated oven for 8 to 10 minutes, depending on the size of the cookies. They should be golden but not too hard. The finished cookies should remain moist and slightly chewy. Let cool on a wire rack. Store in an airtight container when completely cool.

Decadent Chocolate Brownies

THERE'S REALLY ABSOLUTELY NOTHING IRISH ABOUT THIS RICH, FUDGY BROWNIE, BUT WE'VE YET TO MEET AN IRISHMAN WHO DOESN'T FALL FOR IT. BESIDES, EVERY COOKBOOK SHOULD CONTAIN AT LEAST ONE KILLER CHOCOLATE DESSERT RECIPE. **Serves 8** Ⓥ

Preheat the oven to 350 degrees F. Grease a 10-inch square baking pan.

Sift together the flour, confectioners' sugar, and cocoa into a large bowl. Melt the chocolate in the top pan of a double boiler placed over gently simmering water or in a heatproof bowl placed over a saucepan of simmering water. Add the butter and the golden syrup and stir until blended. Leave to cool to lukewarm, then stir in the eggs and vanilla extract. Fold in the flour mixture and stir rather quickly until smooth. Fold in the nuts. Pour the mixture into the prepared pan.

Bake in the preheated oven for 30 to 45 minutes. The top and edges will be crusty. The inside will be slightly gooey but not runny. Remove from the oven and let cool in the pan.

Cut into squares and serve while still warm with a dollop of whipped cream or, even better, vanilla ice cream. This brownie keeps for a couple of days if wrapped completely in plastic wrap.

2/3 cup all-purpose flour

1 1/4 cups confectioners' sugar

4 tablespoons unsweetened cocoa powder

5 ounces semisweet chocolate

7 tablespoons unsalted butter, melted

2 tablespoons golden syrup

2 eggs

1 1/2 teaspoons vanilla extract

4 tablespoons hazelnuts, toasted, skinned, and chopped

whipped cream or vanilla ice cream for serving

CHAPTER FIFTEEN

The Orchard

It is County Armagh that carries the name "the orchard of Ireland," and in fact it wasn't that long ago that every farmhouse had its own orchard of some size, shape, or description. The persistent rain—such an integral part of the Irish climate—allows a great variety of fruit trees to thrive, and if the farm wife tended and nurtured her trees, she was rewarded with the season's bounty. Bramley and cider apples, Conference pears, Victoria plums, and wild cherries all had their place, and every orchard we visited seemed to have a little corner or border reserved for the obliging bushes of raspberries, currants, and gooseberries.

To a chef, especially a pastry chef, each season's harvest has an exciting allure to tempt and tease the taste buds. Spring brings colorful rhubarb and tangy gooseberries. Those long summer days promise sumptuous soft fruits and delicious berries. Autumn is the time for crisp, crunchy apples and moist, juicy pears. With such a vast array of flavors, is it any wonder that a great heritage developed? Passed from mother to daughter, neighbor to friend, a huge repertoire of humble yet pleasing desserts grew up to enhance, to emphasize, to satisfy: from crispy crumbles to silky fools, latticed tarts to double-crust pies, steaming puddings to hearty cakes. From the windfalls and surpluses, the traditions of jam making and preserving ensured a stocked larder throughout the gray winter months.

Not only does the tended fruit flourish, but all sorts of berries proliferate throughout the countryside. Delicate elderberries hedge country lanes, blackberry brambles tumble over County Down drumlins, rowanberries bring bright confusion to the Wicklow hills, the moorland areas offer up bilberries and black currants. It is simply a matter of putting on your boots and the endless bounty is there, waiting to be picked and enjoyed.

White Chocolate and Cherry Trifle

DO NOT BE PUT OFF BY THIS DESSERT THINKING IT SOUNDS COMPLEX AND TIME-CONSUMING. WITH A LITTLE ORGANIZATION, IT CAN BE VERY SIMPLE AND QUICK TO ASSEMBLE. YOU CAN USE ANY CHOCOLATE COOKIES, STORE-BOUGHT OR OTHERWISE, AND THE CHERRIES CAN BE PREPARED DAYS IN ADVANCE AND STORED IN THE REFRIGERATOR. FEEL FREE TO USE FRESH RASPBERRIES OR STRAWBERRIES IF YOU PREFER. WITH A LITTLE CARE, THE PRESENTATION OF THIS DESSERT, IN AN ATTRACTIVE GLASS OR MOLD, LIFTS IT FROM THE REALM OF THE ORDINARY TO THE HEIGHTS OF DINNER-PARTY ELEGANCE. **Serves 4 to 6** Ⓥ

For the biscuit:

2 teaspoons vanilla extract

10 ounces semisweet chocolate, melted and cooled

6 eggs, separated

2/3 cup superfine sugar

For poaching the cherries:

1 bottle (750 ml) full-bodied red wine or port

2 cups water

2 1/4 cups granulated sugar

1 lemon slice

1/2 vanilla bean, split lengthwise

1 pound cherries, pitted

For the white chocolate mousse:

2 eggs

12 ounces white chocolate, melted and cooled slightly

7 tablespoons Vanilla Anglaise (see page 186)

1 3/4 cups whipping cream, whipped to soft peaks

Preheat the oven to 350 degrees F. Grease and line a baking sheet with greased parchment paper.

To make the biscuit, add the vanilla extract to the melted chocolate, then mix in the egg yolks. In a bowl, whisk the egg whites and sugar to form firm, glossy peaks. Fold the egg whites into the chocolate mixture. Spread thinly and evenly onto the prepared baking sheet; it will be about 1/2 inch thick.

Bake in the preheated oven for about 15 minutes, or until the mixture is firm. Let cool on a wire rack. It will sink slightly as it cools. When it is cool, cut out pieces in suitable shapes to line the trifle glass or mold, keeping all the crumbs to use in the base.

To poach the cherries, place the wine or port in a large pan, bring to a boil, and boil until reduced by half. Add all the remaining ingredients, except the cherries, and return to a boil. Place the cherries into the poaching syrup and simmer gently for 10 minutes. Remove from the heat and let cool. (The cherries will have a deeper, richer color if they are left to sit in the syrup overnight. If covered in the syrup, they will keep in the refrigerator for weeks.)

To make the mousse, place the eggs in a heatproof bowl over (but not touching) hot water in a saucepan. Whisk over gentle heat until slightly warmer than body temperature. Remove from the heat and continue to whisk until cool. The eggs will be very light in color and will double in volume.

Slowly add the melted white chocolate, followed by the Vanilla Anglaise, and then the softly whipped cream. This mousse will be quite soft, which is desired for this dessert. Place in the refrigerator for at least 1 hour before assembling the dessert.

Strain the cherries and return the syrup to the pan. Discard the lemon slice and vanilla bean. Boil the syrup until reduced by half to a syrupy consistency. Remove from the heat and let cool.

Put a layer of the chocolate biscuit in the bottom of the trifle glass or mold, along with any crumbs, and soak with 1 to 2 tablespoons of the poaching syrup. Ladle in enough white chocolate mousse to fill the glass by one-third and then add another layer of chocolate biscuit. Again, soak with the syrup and place a generous layer of cherries on top. (If the cherries are large, you may wish to halve them.) Ladle in another layer of mousse and again sprinkle with cherries.

Make curls of semisweet and milk chocolate by shaving them off the block with a peeler. Garnish the top of the trifle with big curls of white and dark chocolate and a few mint leaves. The trifle can be made several hours in advance; if this is the case, do not add the garnish until you are ready to serve.

To garnish:

2 ounces semisweet chocolate

2 ounces white chocolate

a few fresh mint leaves

Amaretti Sablé of Peaches
with a Caramel Cream

THE ALMOND FLAVOR OF THESE BISCUITS MARRIES PERFECTLY WITH PEACHES, ALTHOUGH APRICOTS WOULD BE EQUALLY AT HOME IN THIS DESSERT. BE SURE YOUR FRUIT IS RIPE AND UNBLEMISHED. **Serves 4** (Ⓥ)

4 peaches

eight 3-inch round Amaretti Sablé (see opposite)

For the poaching syrup:

2 cups dry white wine

2 cups water

4 1/2 cups sugar

1 lemon slice

1 orange slice

1/2 vanilla bean, split lengthwise

For the caramel cream:

3/4 cup superfine sugar

5 tablespoons water

3/4 cup plus 2 tablespoons whipping cream

2/3 cup mascarpone cheese

Blanch the peaches for 10 seconds in a large pan of boiling water, and then transfer them to a container full of cold water. Slip off the skins. Combine all the poaching syrup ingredients in a large pan and bring to a boil. Add the peaches and return to a simmer. The cooking time depends on the size and degree of ripeness of the peaches, but usually 5 to 10 minutes will suffice. If you plunge the tip of a very sharp knife into one of the peaches and the tip passes through easily to the pit, they are ready. Remove from the heat and let the peaches cool in the syrup. (This syrup can be strained and kept in the refrigerator for use at another time.)

To make the caramel cream, place the sugar and water in a heavy-bottomed pan, stir to dissolve the sugar, and cook over a high heat without stirring until the mixture is a medium caramel—a nice amber. Remove from the heat and gently stir in the cream. Return to low heat for 1 to 2 minutes to ensure that all the caramel has dissolved into the cream. Strain through a fine-mesh sieve into a bowl and leave to cool. When completely cold, slowly stir in the mascarpone. The result should be a smooth, thick, creamy mixture.

To assemble the dessert, place one of the amaretti on each plate and spread a generous helping of the caramel cream on the cookie. Halve, pit, and slice the peach halves into fan shapes, and arrange them on top of the caramel cream. Gently lay the remaining cookies on top. Garnish with a sprinkling of ground amaretti, if desired.

Amaretti Sablé

SABLÉ—IN FRENCH, LITERALLY "SAND"—REFERS TO THE DELICATE, CRUMBLY TEXTURE THAT IS INHERENT IN THESE RICH, EXQUISITE COOKIES. PAUL ALWAYS MAKES THEM IN THE FOOD PROCESSOR. BASICALLY, THE MIXTURE IS A VERY SHORT SHORTBREAD DUE TO THE LARGE AMOUNTS OF BOTH BUTTER AND SUGAR. I FIND THAT THE GROUND AMARETTI ADD A DELIGHTFUL FLAVOR THAT MARRIES WELL WITH MANY DIFFERENT FRUITS. YOU CAN BUY AMARETTI, WHICH ARE ITALIAN HARD MACAROONS WITH A BITTER ALMOND FLAVOR, IN MOST SUPERMARKETS. **Makes 24 to 36** (V)

Place the flour, ground amaretti, and sugar in a chilled bowl or food processor bowl. Stir or pulse to mix. Add the diced butter and work it into the dry ingredients with your fingertips or a pastry blender, or process until the mixture begins to come together in pea-sized consistency. Stir the yolks and cream together. Add to the bowl or processor and work quickly with fingertips or pulse briefly until the mixture is just coming together into a mass.

Transfer to a cold, clean work surface and work with the heel of your hand until the mixture is well blended and holds together nicely. Do not overwork. Wrap in plastic wrap and chill for at least 1 hour.

On a lightly floured work surface, work with one-fourth of the mixture at a time, leaving the rest in the refrigerator as the mixture softens very quickly. Carefully roll out about 3/8 inch thick, dusting with flour as necessary. Using a cutter the size and shape you desire, cut out cookies and gently place on an ungreased baking sheet. Chill again at this stage for at least 30 minutes. This rest period ensures minimum shrinkage and helps the cookies bake more evenly.

Preheat the oven to 350 degrees F.

Bake in the preheated oven for 8 to 10 minutes, or until lightly golden. Leave to cool just slightly to allow the cookies to harden a little, then gently slide onto a wire rack to cool completely. Store in an airtight container. They will keep for several days.

3 1/4 cups all-purpose flour

4 ounces amaretti, finely ground

3/4 cup superfine sugar

1 1/2 cups (12 ounces) plus 4 tablespoons unsalted butter, chilled and diced

2 egg yolks

2 tablespoons whipping cream

Spiced Ginger Cake
with Rhubarb Compote

THIS MOIST AND TASTY CAKE COULD BE PAIRED JUST AS EASILY WITH A PLUM COMPOTE, CHUNKY APPLE SAUCE, OR EVEN FRESH RIPE PEARS. **Serves 8 to 10** Ⓥ

For the cake:

3/4 cup (6 ounces) unsalted butter

1/2 cup firmly packed dark brown sugar

2 tablespoons freshly grated ginger root

4 egg yolks, lightly beaten

1 3/4 cups all-purpose flour

1 tablespoon ground ginger

1/2 teaspoon freshly grated nutmeg

1/4 teaspoon ground cloves

1 1/2 teaspoons baking soda

3/4 cup plus 2 tablespoons molasses

7 tablespoons sour cream

8 egg whites

3 tablespoons superfine sugar

For the rhubarb compote:

2 1/4 pounds rhubarb

1 cup superfine sugar

juice of 1 lemon

2 tablespoons grenadine syrup

whipped cream for serving (optional)

Preheat the oven to 350 degrees F. Butter a 9- or 10-inch springform pan. In a bowl, beat together the butter, brown sugar, and fresh ginger until light and fluffy. Slowly add the egg yolks, mixing continuously.

In another bowl, sift together the flour, ground ginger, nutmeg, cloves, and baking soda. Stir together the molasses and sour cream in yet another bowl. Fold the flour mixture and molasses mixture alternately into the egg yolk mixture. Whisk together the egg whites and superfine sugar until glossy peaks form. Fold into the cake batter. Mix until no white streaks remain. Pour into the prepared pan.

Bake in the preheated oven for about 45 minutes, or until the cake sides are pulling away from the pan and a skewer inserted into the center comes out clean. Remove from the oven, let cool for 10 minutes, then release the pan sides. Let cool completely on a wire rack. (The cake can be kept wrapped in plastic wrap for 2 to 3 days.)

Finally, make the compote: If the rhubarb stalks are large, peel them to remove any strings. Chop into 3/4-inch dice and place in a large heavy-bottomed pan with the superfine sugar and lemon juice. Cook over gentle heat, stirring occasionally to prevent sticking. When the rhubarb is getting soft but not mushy, remove from the heat. Pour into a bowl to stop the cooking.

Depending on the rhubarb, a certain amount of liquid will have been released. If there seems to be too much in comparison to the amount of fruit, drain some off. Add the grenadine and stir in gently. This turns the compote a lovely pink. The compote keeps well in an airtight container in the refrigerator.

Serve each wedge of cake with a ladle of compote beside it. A dollop of cream finishes it nicely.

Brandy Snaps

THIS CRISP, DELICATE, LACEY-LOOKING COOKIE CAN BE SHAPED IN VARIOUS WAYS DEPENDING ON THE INTENDED USE. IT CAN BE SERVED ON ITS OWN OR AS AN ACCOMPANIMENT. IF YOU LIKE, YOU CAN FREEZE THE BATTER TO USE LATER. **Makes about 24** (V)

In a bowl, beat together the butter and sugar until light and fluffy.

Heat the golden syrup gently until just warm enough to be in a more liquid state. This allows it to mix in better with the other ingredients. Slowly add to the butter-sugar mixture. Obviously, if it is too warm it will cause the butter to melt, and this should be avoided. Slowly work in the flour and ginger, if using, and then place in the refrigerator for at least 1 hour.

Preheat the oven to 400 degrees F. Butter a baking sheet.

When ready to bake, pat out spoonfuls of the batter, using damp fingers, into rounds about 1 1/4 inches in diameter. Place on the prepared baking sheet, leaving lots of room between to allow for spreading. Don't try to cook more than a few at a time because after they are cooked and cooled slightly, they will only stay malleable for seconds.

Bake in the preheated oven for 3 to 5 minutes, or until they have spread, gone lacy, and turned a deep golden brown. Remove from the oven and do not touch for about 1 minute. They need this time to start to set. Using a palette knife, lift and quickly shape each cookie as desired. The inside of a bowl gives a lovely basket shape in which to serve scoops of ice cream. Wrap around a wooden or metal cylinder to get a "cannoli" shape, or form into a horn shape by holding one edge tightly on the end of a sharpening steel and letting the other edge fan out. If the cookies harden before you have shaped them, just return them to the oven for a few seconds and they will again soften.

These cookies will stay crisp and fresh for a couple of days if stored in an airtight container.

1/2 cup (4 ounces) plus 1 tablespoon unsalted butter

rounded 1 cup superfine sugar

1/2 cup golden syrup

scant 1 cup all-purpose flour

a pinch of ground ginger (optional)

Apple Tart
with a Walnut Crumble Topping

THE BRAMLEY, AN IRISH FAVORITE, IS CONSIDERED BY MANY TO BE THE WORLD'S BEST COOKING APPLE. ANY GOOD COOKING APPLE—GOLDEN DELICIOUS, ROME BEAUTY, WINESAP—CAN BE SUBSTITUTED. **Serves 8** (V)

1/4 recipe Sweet Shortcrust Pastry (see page 184)

2 egg yolks, lightly beaten

For the filling:

8 to 10 Bramley apples or other good cooking apples, about 1 1/4 pounds (see note)

grated zest and juice of 1 lemon

scant 2/3 cup superfine sugar

2 teaspoons ground cinnamon

4 tablespoons unsalted butter

1 1/2 teaspoons corn starch

For the crumble:

1/3 cup granulated sugar

6 tablespoons brown sugar

4 tablespoons all-purpose flour

1 teaspoon ground cinnamon

3/4 walnuts, toasted and chopped

4 tablespoons unsalted butter, chilled and diced

whipped cream or crème fraîche for serving

Preheat the oven to 375 degrees F. Butter a 9- or 10-inch tart pan with a removable bottom. On a lightly floured work surface, roll out the pastry 1/8 inch thick. Fit it into the prepared pan, trimming the edges even. Place in the refrigerator to chill for 30 minutes.

Line the pastry-lined pan with parchment paper (or aluminum foil) and fill with pie weights or dried beans. Bake blind in the preheated oven for about 20 minutes until nice and golden. Remove the weights and paper. Brush the inside lightly with the egg yolk.

To make the filling, peel, core, and roughly chop the apples. Place in a bowl and toss with the lemon juice. Sprinkle the lemon zest, sugar, and cinnamon over the apples and mix in.

Melt the butter in a large frying pan over medium heat. Add the apple mixture and cook, stirring frequently, until the apples turn to mush, almost all the juices have evaporated, and the filling is fairly dry. Stir in corn starch. Taste and adjust with more sugar if needed, but remember, the topping is sweet. Remove from the heat.

Place all the crumble ingredients together in a bowl or food processor and rub together with your fingertips or pulse until pea-sized pieces form. Do not overprocess or the butter will start to melt and the topping will be heavy. Refrigerate until needed.

Raise the oven temperature to 400 degrees F. To assemble, spoon a generous amount of apple filling into the base, taking care not to let it fall over the edge of the pan. Sprinkle lots of the topping over the apple filling, but again, take care to avoid the edges of the tart. Bake in the preheated oven for about 15 minutes, or until the topping is cooked, looking golden, and crisp. Remove from the oven and let cool.

Serve warm with whipped cream or crème fraîche.

Deep-Dish Apple Pie

EVERYONE LOVES APPLE PIE. IT IS ONE OF THOSE HUMBLE, COMFORTING DESSERTS THAT IS ALWAYS WELCOME, ESPECIALLY ON CHILLY EVENINGS. **Serves 4** (v)

1 pound Sweet Shortcrust Pastry (see page 184)

2 1/4 pounds Newtown Pippin, Gala, or other good cooking apples

juice of 2 lemons

grated zest of 1 lemon

2 cups sour cream

2 whole eggs

1 2/3 cups superfine sugar

1 tablespoon vanilla extract

2/3 cup all-purpose flour

2 egg yolks, lightly beaten

crème fraîche, whipped cream, or cinnamon ice cream for serving

On a lightly floured board, roll out the pastry 1/8 inch thick. Cut into 2 rounds, one about 10 inches in diameter and the other 11 to 12 inches in diameter. Chill for 30 minutes.

Peel, core, and finely slice the apples. Place in a bowl and toss with the lemon juice. Set aside. Stir together the lemon zest, sour cream, whole eggs, superfine sugar, vanilla extract, and flour in a separate bowl until smooth and homogeneous.

Butter a pie dish with deep, sloping sides. Fit the smaller pastry round into it and chill again for 30 minutes.

Preheat the oven to 350 degrees F. Brush the base of the tart with some of the beaten egg yolk. This helps to seal the pastry, thus preventing it from getting too soggy during baking.

Toss the apples with the sour cream filling and pile the whole mixture into the pie dish, heaping it into a generous dome. The sour cream mixture will set as it cooks, so do pour it all in as long as it does not overflow the sides.

Take the second pastry round from the refrigerator. Brush the perimeter of the pastry base with the egg yolk, and gently lay the pastry round on the top, sealing the edges of the pastry together. Trim the edges so that a sealed margin of about 3/4 inch is left. This margin can then be pinched into a decorative shape with thumb and forefinger. With a knife tip, slit the top crust in a few places to allow the steam to escape during cooking and brush the surface with the egg yolk. This will turn nice and shiny golden as it bakes.

Bake in the preheated oven for 45 to 55 minutes. The pastry should be firm and golden and the apple slices should pierce easily with a skewer. Remove from the oven and leave to cool. Serve when just warm with a big scoop of crème fraîche, whipped cream, or cinnamon ice cream.

Honey and Ginger Ice Cream
with a Plum Compote

NOTHING BEATS HOMEMADE ICE CREAM. USING QUALITY INGREDIENTS ENSURES THAT. WE ALWAYS USE AN ICE CREAM MACHINE, AS ONE CANNOT QUITE REPRODUCE THE SAME QUALITY BY HAND. FRUIT COMPOTES PROVIDE AN EXCELLENT ACCOMPANIMENT. THEY CAN ALSO BE A DESSERT IN THEIR OWN RIGHT, WITH JUST A DOLLOP OF FRESH CREAM. **Serves 6 to 8** Ⓥ

For the ice cream:

2 1/4 cups milk

2 1/4 cups whipping cream

2 tablespoons chopped fresh root ginger

1/2 vanilla bean, split lengthwise

12 egg yolks

3/4 cup superfine sugar

7 tablespoons honey

chopped candied ginger

For the plum compote:

2 pounds plums, halved and pitted

about 2 cups granulated sugar, depending on the tartness of the plums

1/2 vanilla bean, split lengthwise

1/2 cinnamon stick

1 orange slice

Brandy Snaps shaped into baskets (see page 167), optional

fresh mint leaves

To make the ice cream, combine the milk, cream, fresh ginger, and vanilla bean in a large pan. Bring to a boil, then remove from the heat and leave to infuse for 1 hour.

In a bowl, whisk together the egg yolks and superfine sugar until light and fluffy. Return the milk mixture to a boil and then, whisking continuously, pour the milk mixture into the egg yolk mixture. Return the whole mixture to the pan over low heat, and stir continuously with a wooden spoon until it thickens enough to coat the back of the spoon. If you draw your finger across it, it will hold the line on the spoon. If it does not hold the line, it has not cooked enough. Remove from the heat when the right consistency has been reached and strain through a fine-mesh sieve. Stir in the honey, and leave to cool.

Transfer the cooled custard to an ice cream machine and freeze according to the manufacturer's instructions. Alternatively, pour into a freezer container and place in the freezer until firm, whisking every 30 minutes to break up the ice crystals.

Candied ginger can either be sprinkled into the ice cream during the final churning or whisking or reserved as a garnish to sprinkle over it.

To make the plum compote, combine all the ingredients in a large, heavy-bottomed pan and place over low to medium heat. Taking care that the sugar does not burn on the bottom, cook the compote for 10 to 20 minutes, carefully stirring occasionally and trying not to mash the plums. The timing will depend on the size and ripeness of the plums. They should be soft but still hold their shape. Remove from the heat and leave to cool in the juices released during cooking.

There is usually a lot of liquid released. Strain this off into a pan and boil until reduced by half to concentrate the flavor. However, if it is reduced too much, it tends to be bitter, so taste regularly to check for this. You may find that you only want to add a little of this liquid back to the plums, depending on what you are then using them for.

Meanwhile, with the tip of a sharp knife, the job of skinning the plums should now be relatively easy. These plums can be kept in halves, quarters, or chopped roughly, depending on what the compote is going to be used for. Return them to the reduced liquid. The compote keeps very well in the refrigerator in a sealed container.

Serve the ice cream in a cookie basket, if desired. Scatter the candied ginger over the top, if it has not been added to the ice cream. Surround the ice cream with the plum compote and garnish the compote with mint leaves.

Plum Clafoutis

THIS FRENCH SPECIALTY, WHICH TRADITIONALLY CALLS FOR CHERRIES, CAN BE EASILY ADAPTED TO PLUMS OR OTHER FRUITS. A THINNER-SKINNED PLUM SUCH AS A GREENGAGE IS DESIRABLE. **Serves 6** Ⓥ

Preheat the oven to 350 degrees F.

Grease a shallow oven dish with the butter. Place the plum halves, cut side down and fairly tightly together, over the bottom of the dish. Sift together the flour, salt, and superfine sugar. Slowly mix in the eggs by hand, followed by the milk. Do not mix excessively, as this type of batter can be toughened by too much handling. Beat in the yolks and almond and vanilla extracts. Pour the batter over the plums.

Bake in the preheated oven for about 40 minutes, or until the batter has risen and is golden brown. Remove from the oven and dust liberally with confectioners' sugar.

1 tablespoon unsalted butter

1 pound plums, halved and pitted

3 1/2 tablespoons pastry flour

pinch of salt

4 to 6 tablespoons superfine sugar, or more if plums are very tart

2 eggs

1 1/2 cups milk

2 egg yolks

1 or 2 drops almond extract

2 teaspoons vanilla extract

confectioners' sugar

Apple Tarte Tatin
with Apple Sorbet

TARTE TATIN IS A FRENCH CLASSIC THAT NEVER SEEMS TO GO OUT OF STYLE. FOR THE BEST RESULTS, WE ALWAYS USE A FOOD PROCESSOR TO MAKE SORBETS. **Serves 6** (V)

For the tart:

about 9 ounces Puff Pastry (see page 182)

12 to 16 crisp, tart apples such as Granny Smith or pippin

juice of 2 lemons

1/2 cup (4 ounces) plus 3 tablespoons unsalted butter, at room temperature

3/4 to 1 cup superfine sugar, less for a sweeter apple, more for a tarter one

For the sorbet:

2 cups plus 2 tablespoons dry apple cider

2 cups superfine sugar

grated zest and juice of 1 lemon

1 1/8 pounds good cooking apples such as Bramley (an Irish favorite), Rome Beauty, or Winesap, peeled, cored, and chopped

Preheat the oven to 400 degrees F.

To make the tart, on a lightly floured board, roll out the pastry into a round about 1/8 inch thick. It must be no thicker than 1/4 inch or the tart will not cook properly. Chill this round in the refrigerator for at least 30 minutes.

Meanwhile, peel, core, and halve the apples. Place in a large bowl and toss with the lemon juice.

Select a medium-sized, heavy-bottomed, ovenproof, low-sided pan. Using a spatula, spread the butter evenly all over the base. Sprinkle on all the sugar, again distributing evenly. Starting at the perimeter, arrange the apple halves on their side in a pinwheel fashion, filling the middle after a full circle of halves is in place. These need to be quite tightly packed or they will fall over in the cooking process.

Place the pan over high heat. Watching that no part of the butter-sugar layer starts to burn or blacken, cook until it has turned golden and caramel. At this point, you may want to squeeze in one more apple half to ensure that they all stay upright. This part of the cooking process will take about 15 minutes, depending on the heat.

Carefully lay the chilled round of pastry on top of the apples, tucking in the edges and turning them down so that when the tart is inverted, the edges will create a rim that will hold in the apple juices and caramel. Place the pan in the preheated oven for about 20 minutes to cook the puff pastry as well as to finish cooking the apples.

Remove from the oven and, taking great care, loosen the edges of the tart with a knife. Lay a plate or tray that is larger than the pan on top and quickly invert the pan and plate at the same time so that the tart turns out onto the plate. With a palette knife, pat any apples that have loosened back into place and leave to cool. All the juices will be reabsorbed and the caramel will set slightly because of the pectin released from the apples.

To make the sorbet, put the cider, sugar, lemon zest, and juice in a large pan. Place the chopped apples into the liquid and simmer gently, stirring occasionally, until the apples are completely cooked and mushy. Be careful that the sugar all dissolves and doesn't catch on the bottom of the pan.

Rub the mixture through a conical sieve or other fine-mesh sieve and let cool. Taste again to adjust the flavoring, as this can vary depending on the apples. It might need a little more sugar, lemon juice, or even cider. You are aiming for a slightly tart, tangy taste, not too sweet, to balance the richness of the tart.

Transfer to an ice cream machine and freeze according to the manufacturer's instructions. Alternatively, spoon into a freezer container and freeze until firm, whisking every 30 minutes to break up the ice crystals. (This sorbet can be served on its own as well.)

To assemble the dessert, cut the tart into wedges and present on slightly warmed plates. Place a spoonful of sorbet at the side. (This dessert does not keep well, but don't worry. There is rarely any left).

Basic Recipes

Most of the recipes listed here are ones that are referred to several times in this book, but this is by no means a complete guide to basic recipes. We would, however, encourage any serious cook to familiarize themselves totally with them. Serious cooks should compile their own guide, from stocks and sauces to pastas, pastries, and so on. It is only through a complete understanding of the basics that a cook can become free of the need for recipes. Just as professional musicians, for example, have a strong foundation of classical techniques behind them, so a knowledge of basic methods must become ingrained in a cook. With this knowledge and understanding, one has the ability to foresee possible disasters or to correct and rescue any accidents. More importantly, though, one can then move on to invent sparklingly new and original dishes.

Vinaigrette Dressing

THERE ARE ENDLESS VARIATIONS THAT COME UNDER THE DEFINITION OF VINAIGRETTE. BASICALLY, A LOT OF WHAT GOES INTO THE DRESSING DEPENDS UPON PERSONAL TASTE AND WHAT THE VINAIGRETTE IS GOING TO DRESS. A GOOD RATIO TO WORK FROM IS ONE PART VINEGAR TO FOUR OR FIVE PARTS OIL. FOR THOSE WHO ARE ALLERGIC TO VINEGAR, LEMON JUICE IS A GOOD SUBSTITUTE. **Makes about 1 cup** (V)

Dissolve the salt, pepper, and mustard in the wine vinegar in a bowl. Whisk in the oil, slowly at first to allow it to be incorporated. Taste and adjust the seasoning as needed. This can easily be made in a blender. Simply place all the ingredients in together and blend.

Keep all vinaigrettes in the refrigerator if they are not being used immediately, otherwise they can develop a rancid taste.

1/2 teaspoon salt

1/2 teaspoon freshly ground black pepper

2 teaspoons Dijon mustard

2 to 4 tablespoons white wine vinegar

1 cup less 1 tablespoon olive or vegetable oil

Mayonnaise

YOU CAN VARY THIS RECIPE WITH THE ADDITION OF A FAVORITE HERB, SUCH AS BASIL OR PARSLEY.
Serves 4 (V)

Whisk the mustard, salt and pepper to taste, and vinegar in a bowl until the salt has dissolved. Add the egg yolks and combine well. Then whisk in the oil, very slowly at first, literally drop by drop. As the mayonnaise starts to build up, you can add the oil slightly faster, but always be sure to incorporate each addition fully before adding more. Continue until you have blended in all the oil and the mayonnaise is thick and creamy.

1 tablespoon Dijon mustard

salt and freshly ground white pepper

1 tablespoon white wine vinegar

3 egg yolks

2 cups plus 2 tablespoons vegetable or light olive oil

Brown Chicken Stock

BROWN CHICKEN STOCK IS INVALUABLE TO BOTH THE PROFESSIONAL AND THE HOME CHEF. FOR CONVENIENCE, MAKE IT IN LARGE BATCHES. IT CAN BE BOILED DOWN TO CONCENTRATE THE FLAVORS, AND THEN FROZEN SO IT IS ALWAYS ON HAND. **Makes about 3 1/2 quarts** ⓥ

7 pounds chicken bones, wings, and legs

1 pound onions, chopped

1 pound carrots, chopped

7 ounces celery, chopped

1 whole garlic bulb

1/2 cup tomato paste

1 Bouquet Garni (see page 188)

Preheat the oven to 400 degrees F.

Chop the chicken bones and pieces with a heavy knife. Place in a roasting pan and roast in the preheated oven for about 30 minutes, or until nicely brown. Add the onions, carrots, celery, and garlic and roast for another 10 minutes.

Transfer the bones and vegetables to a large pot and fill with cold water by several inches. Bring to a boil and skim off any fat and scum. Add the tomato paste and Bouquet Garni. Cover and simmer for 2 hours, skimming frequently. Strain through a fine-mesh sieve.

If you want a thicker, stronger stock, reduce the stock by boiling, or thicken with a little of your favorite gravy thickener.

Store in an airtight container in the refrigerator or in lock-top plastic bags in the freezer.

Gourmet Pizza Dough

THIS EGG-ENRICHED DOUGH IS LIGHTER THAN THE TRADITIONAL PIZZA DOUGH, SO IT MAKES A GREAT STARTER OR SNACK. IF YOU HAVE A MIXER OR FOOD PROCESSOR, YOU CAN TAKE SOME OF THE HARD WORK OUT OF THE KNEADING PROCESS. **Makes six 7-inch rounds** Ⓥ

Combine the yeast with the warm water and leave for about 10 minutes until frothy and foamy.

Place the flour and salt in a bowl. Add the yeast mixture, the eggs, and the butter and mix until the ingredients form a dough. Knead the dough on a lightly floured work surface until it is shiny, elastic, and smooth. Place in a greased bowl, cover with oiled plastic wrap, and leave to rise in a warm place for about 2 hours, or until doubled in size.

Grease 3 baking sheets.

Lightly flour the work surface and tip out the dough onto it. Divide into 6 equal portions. With a rolling pin, work each portion into a round 7 to 8 inches in diameter. The dough will be about 1/4 inch thick. With your fingertips, neatly fold up the edges to give a nice rim to the dough round. Place on the prepared baking sheet, and finish the other pieces in the same way. Cover with oiled plastic wrap and again leave to rise; this time it will only take about 30 minutes.

Preheat the oven to 400 to 425 degrees F.

Bake in the preheated oven for about 10 minutes, or until light golden brown. Remove from the oven and let cool on a wire rack.

These can be used immediately to make individual-sized gourmet pizzas or wrapped completely in plastic wrap and placed in the refrigerator or freezer until needed.

scant 1 tablespoon active dry yeast (1 package) or 1/2 ounce fresh yeast

1/2 cup warm water (about 104 degrees F)

2 1/3 cups all-purpose flour

a pinch of salt

2 eggs, lightly beaten

4 tablespoons butter, diced and at room temperature

Pasta Dough

MAKING PASTA IS A SIMPLE, YET SATISFYING PROCEDURE. THE DOUGH CAN BE FROZEN UNTIL IT IS NEEDED, SO MAKE IT UP IN BIG BATCHES. DO EXPERIMENT BY ADDING HERBS OR SPICES. THEY OFFER A WHOLE NEW RANGE OF FLAVORS. ONCE YOU'VE TRIED FRESH PASTA, YOU'LL BE HOOKED! **Serves 6 as a starter, or 4 as a main course** Ⓥ

1 3/4 to 2 1/8 cups all-purpose flour or extra-fine semolina flour, or half of each

3 eggs

a pinch of salt

1 tablespoon olive oil

Mound the flour in center of a work surface. Make a well in the middle and place the eggs, salt, and oil in the well. Gradually, using one hand, incorporate the flour from the edges into the liquid, stirring and mixing until a stiff dough forms.

Knead this dough for 5 to 10 minutes, or until shiny, smooth, and elastic. If it is too soft, add a little more flour. If it seems too dry, add a spoonful of water. These basic ingredients will react together depending on factors such as temperature and humidity, so the results will vary. Once the dough is ready, it must rest. Wrap it in plastic wrap and place in the refrigerator for at least 30 minutes. All this can be done in a stand mixer with a dough hook or even in a food processor. If made in a machine, extend the resting time to 1 hour.

When it comes to rolling out the dough, the most efficient way is with one of the many hand-cranked machines that are widely available. However, people have done it by hand for hundreds of years, so don't feel intimidated. On a floured surface, work with one-fourth of the dough at a time. With a rolling pin, roll out the dough as thinly as possible, aiming for it to be less than 1/8 inch thick—basically, as thin as possible. Once this has been achieved, it is simply a matter of cutting it into the required shape: narrow strips, wide strips, or whatever you choose.

If using a machine, again take just one-fourth of the dough at a time and work it through the rollers, taking it thinner each time until it is the desired thinness, usually the last or second-to-last setting.

The secret to cooking pasta uniformly and without it all sticking together is to use lots of salted boiling water. A general rule of thumb is to use about 1 quart of water for every 4 ounces of pasta. Adding a tablespoon of oil to the water is also a common recommendation. The length of cooking time will be dependent on the type and size of the noodles.

They should be tender but still have a slight bite. Thin strips of fresh pasta will only take 3 to 4 minutes. Taste to see when the pasta is cooked. When it is ready, drain it into a colander and use immediately.

Ravioli:

This dough must stay slightly softer to make shaping the ravioli easier. To achieve this, follow the basic pasta dough recipe, but add 1 egg yolk. This will result is a softer, more malleable dough that will not dry out as quickly, and it will not crack or break once shaped.

Pasta Nera:

This black dough gets its color from the ink sac of a cuttlefish (or several sacs from several smaller squid). Again, a slight alteration to the basic dough is needed. Omit 1 whole egg from the recipe and substitute 5 tablespoons of ink from the ink sac. Be sure to add the ink by first passing it through a fine sieve. It may also be necessary to add more flour, up to 1/3 cup or more. Mix this dough in a large bowl rather than on a work surface because it can get very messy. The ink can also be purchased in plastic pouches in specialty food shops.

Savory Shortcrust Pastry

JUST FLOUR, WATER, AND BUTTER CAN PRODUCE A SATISFACTORY RESULT, BUT I LIKE TO ENRICH THIS SHORTCRUST WITH EGGS AND CREAM. YOU CAN MAKE THE PASTRY BY HAND OR IN A FOOD PROCESSOR.

Makes about 2 pounds (V)

Place the flour, sugar, and salt in a chilled bowl. Rub in the butter with your fingertips or a pastry blender until the mixture forms pea-sized lumps.

3 2/3 cups all-purpose flour

1 1/2 tablespoons sugar

2 teaspoons salt

1 1/2 cups (12 ounces) plus 2 tablespoons unsalted butter, chilled and diced

2 eggs

2 tablespoons light cream

In another bowl, stir together the eggs and cream. Pour into the flour mixture and mix until the ingredients come together in a dough. Transfer to a work surface and, using the heel of your hand, work together until the mixture holds together nicely. It should now be wrapped in plastic wrap and chilled for at least 1 hour. This firms up the butter and allows the gluten in the flour to relax.

Divide into 3 portions, wrap well, and store in the refrigerator for up to a week or in the freezer for up to a month.

Puff Pastry

JEANNE WAS TAUGHT THIS PUFF PASTRY RECIPE WHEN SHE WORKED FOR ALBERT ROUX. ALTHOUGH SHE HAS SINCE TRIED MANY OTHER RECIPES, THIS IS THE ONE SHE KEEPS COMING BACK TO. PUFF PASTRY MUST BE AMONG THE MOST REWARDING PASTRIES TO MAKE. YOU BEGIN WITH THE MOST BASIC OF INGREDIENTS, YET WITH TIME AND A GENTLE TOUCH YOU END UP WITH THE MOST DELIGHTFUL RESULTS. YOU CAN MAKE THE PASTRY BY HAND OR IN A STAND MIXER OR FOOD PROCESSOR. **Makes just over 2 1/4 pounds** (V)

3 2/3 cups bread flour

6 tablespoons (3 ounces) unsalted butter

1 tablespoon salt

1 egg yolk

1 cup less 1 tablespoon water

1 tablespoon white wine vinegar

1 1/3 pounds (21 ounces) unsalted butter, diced

1 1/4 cups all-purpose flour

Place the first batch of flour (3 2/3 cups) together with the first batch of butter (6 tablespoons) and the salt in a bowl and rub in the butter with your fingertips or a pastry blender until the mixture resembles coarse meal.

Stir together the yolk, water, and wine vinegar and add them to the bowl. Mix the ingredients together for a good 5 to 10 minutes until they all come together into a smooth, shiny dough. Wrap in plastic wrap and place in the refrigerator to rest for 1 hour.

Now place the larger batch of butter with the second batch of flour (1 1/4 cups) into a bowl and mix to a smooth pastelike consistency. Do not mix too much or the butter will get too soft and start to melt. Tip out onto a work surface. Pat into a neat rectangle and wrap in plastic wrap. Place in the refrigerator for 1 hour.

After 1 hour, remove both batches. Place the flour-based dough on a floured work surface. Roll it out into a 12-inch square. Place the butter-based paste in the center of the dough and gently, without stretching, fold all 4 sides over as if wrapping the butter-based dough like a present. The object is to enclose the butter completely so that when you start to roll the dough out, none of the butter can escape or leak out.

Roll the "package" out gently but surely until you have a rectangle measuring about 8 by 18 inches. Brush off any excess flour and fold up the bottom third, then fold down the top third. Turn this rectangle so it is lengthwise on the work surface and again roll out to the same dimensions. Fold into thirds again, the way you would a business letter, wrap in plastic wrap, and place in the refrigerator to chill and rest for 1 hour. This chilling and resting stage is of vital importance. The ingredients must stay cool or their properties will change, and your puff pastry would not end up with the right results.

After 1 hour, remove from the refrigerator and roll out twice more in exactly the same way as before. All this rolling is how the many layers that are in puff pastry are formed. If the puff dough is allowed to get too soft, and is forced too much, these layers will be damaged. Wrap in plastic wrap and return to the refrigerator to rest again for 1 hour.

The last rolling is only one turn, not two like the previous two times. This is the classic amount of rolls and turns given to puff pastry. After it has again rested and chilled, it is ready to use. This puff freezes well, so if you are going to go to all the effort of making it, be sure to make at least this quantity and then you will have some in the freezer, on hand, when you need it.

To roll out the pastry, take one-fourth of the total dough to roll at a time. Place on a floured work surface and with a rolling pin, gently work it out to a thickness of about 1/4 inch. This thickness, when cooked, will rise to a good 2 inches. Place the sheet of puff pastry onto a baking sheet and chill for at least 20 minutes before cutting into the desired shapes.

To bake the puff pastry, place the cut pieces on a slightly dampened baking sheet (by being damp the puff will stay in place and not slide all over when you go to brush it with an egg wash).

Usually puff pieces are brushed on top with an egg wash. This is what gives them the lovely golden and shiny appearance when cooked. This also allows you to decorate the top if you desire, by gently "drawing" simple designs onto the egg wash.

Puff pastry needs to be cooked in a hot oven to puff up properly. Put it in at about 400 degrees F. The temperature can be turned down after the first 10 minutes to 350 to 375 degrees F, and then the cooking is continued for another 10 to 15 minutes. This ensures that the puff piece is cooked right through and that the middle won't be a soggy mass of uncooked dough.

Sweet Shortcrust Pastry

THIS SHORTCRUST IS A CRISP YET TENDER PASTRY THAT IS VERY WORKABLE. THE MORE SUGAR A SHORTCRUST DOUGH HAS, THE "SHORTER" AND HARDER TO WORK WITH IT BECOMES. THE SECRET IS TO REMEMBER TO KEEP EVERYTHING COOL, BOTH INGREDIENTS AND THE BOWL. CHILL FOR 20 TO 30 MINUTES BEFORE ROLLING, AND THE SAME AGAIN AFTER ROLLING AND LINING THE TART PAN. THIS WILL GIVE THE BEST RESULTS BECAUSE THE BUTTER WILL NOT HAVE THE OPPORTUNITY TO MELT, WHICH TENDS TO MAKE THE PASTRY HEAVY AND DENSE. IT IS WORTH MAKING THIS DOUGH IN THE QUANTITY GIVEN HERE—IT IS ESPECIALLY EASY IN A LARGE FOOD PROCESSOR—AND THEN FREEZING WHAT YOU DON'T USE.

Makes four 9- to 10-inch rounds (V)

4 2/3 cups all-purpose flour

3/4 cup superfine sugar

a pinch of salt

1 1/2 cups (12 ounces) unsalted butter

3 eggs, lightly beaten

Place the flour, sugar, and salt in a chilled bowl. Rub in the butter with your fingertips or a pastry blender until the mixture forms pea-sized lumps. Add the eggs and mix until it all starts to mass together.

Transfer the mixture to a floured work surface and, using the heel of your hand, work the mixture until it all holds together in a cohesive ball and there are no big lumps of butter unmixed. Divide into 4 equal portions and wrap well in plastic wrap. Place in the refrigerator. This pastry will keep in the refrigerator for about 1 week and in the freezer for about 1 month.

Blind Baking:

Many recipes call for blind baking a tart base. This is simply a prebaking of the pastry shell. It is accomplished by lining the pastry-lined tart pan with parchment paper or aluminum foil and filling with pie weights or dried beans. This "holds" the pastry in place until it is cooked enough to be set. The pastry is then placed in a preheated oven set at 350 degrees F for about 15 minutes. Often, after removing the weights and paper, the tart shell is popped back into the oven for a minute or two to ensure that the bottom is evenly cooked to a golden brown.

Crème Fraîche

IT IS LIGHT AND LIVELY, AND LESS CLOYING THAN NORMAL CREAM. IT ALSO HAS A LOWER FAT CONTENT AND IT DOESN'T CURDLE EASILY. IT IS SIMPLE TO MAKE. **Makes about 2 cups** Ⓥ

Mix the two ingredients together. Bring to a temperature of 77 to 84 degrees F, no hotter really than a warm room. Cover and let stand at room temperature for 8 to 24 hours. The longer it sits, the more pronounced the tangy flavor. After 24 hours, store, covered, in the refrigerator. It will keep for 7 to 10 days.

2 cups plus 2 tablespoons whipping cream

1 tablespoon buttermilk

Chocolate Almond Cream

IF PREFERRED, THIS RECIPE CAN BE MADE WITHOUT THE CHOCOLATE, ADDING A LITTLE RUM OR VANILLA EXTRACT TO FLAVOR IT INSTEAD. **Makes about 2 pounds** Ⓥ

In a bowl, beat together the butter and sugar until light and fluffy. Add the flour and then the ground almonds. Mix well. Slowly add the eggs, a little at a time, ensuring that they blend in well. Finally, pour in the melted chocolate.

This mixture, stored in a sealed container, can be kept in the refrigerator for several days. It is a real standby filling for fruit tarts and the famous classic puff pastry dessert, pithivier.

1 cup (8 ounces) plus 2 tablespoons unsalted butter

1 1/4 cups superfine sugar

4 tablespoons all-purpose flour

2 1/4 cups ground almonds

4 eggs, lightly beaten

7 ounces semisweet chocolate, melted and cooled

Walnut Shortbread

IF YOU USE A FOOD PROCESSOR OR MIXER, BE CAREFUL NOT TO OVERPROCESS OR THE BUTTER WILL START TO MELT. **Makes 2 rounds of 12 portions, or twenty-four to thirty-six 2-inch rounds or squares** ⓥ

4 cups plus 2 tablespoons all-purpose flour

3/4 cup plus 2 tablespoons sugar

1 1/4 cups walnuts, toasted and ground

1 pound unsalted butter, chilled and diced

Place all the ingredients in a chilled bowl. Using your fingertips or a pastry blender, rub in the butter until the mixture just comes together. Tip out onto a clean work surface and quickly, using the heel of your hand, make sure that all the ingredients are well mixed. Pat into a round, wrap tightly in plastic wrap film, and place in the refrigerator for 1 hour.

On a lightly floured work surface, roll out the chilled piece of dough to a thickness of no more than 1/2 inch. Either form it into 2 rounds and then cut the rounds into pie-type wedges, or if preferred, work into a rectangle and then cut into pieces as desired. Either way, transfer to a baking sheet and chill again for at least 30 minutes.

Preheat the oven to 300 degrees F. Bake the shortbread in the preheated oven for 25 to 30 minutes. Ideally the shortbread should take on little or no color. Allow to cool and set slightly before transferring to a wire rack to finish cooling. Store in an airtight container.

Vanilla Anglaise

THIS IS OUR RECIPE FOR THE STANDARD ENGLISH CUSTARD SAUCE, OR AS THE FRENCH CALL IT, CRÈME ANGLAISE. SILKY AND SMOOTH, IT ENHANCES MOST PUDDINGS AND DESSERTS. **Makes about 2 cups** ⓥ

2 cups plus 2 tablespoons milk, or half milk and half whipping cream

1/2 vanilla bean, split lengthwise, or 1/2 teaspoon vanilla extract

6 egg yolks

2/3 cup superfine sugar

Place the milk in a saucepan with the vanilla bean or extract and bring to a boil. Set aside to let the vanilla infuse.

Whisk the yolks and sugar together in a bowl until lightened in color and the sugar has dissolved. Whisking continuously, slowly pour the hot milk into the yolk-sugar mixture, blending well.

Pour this mixture back into a clean saucepan and cook over low heat. Stir continuously with a wooden spoon until the mixture coats the back of the spoon. Strain the mixture through a fine-mesh sieve and let cool. If you have used the vanilla bean, you can leave it in the sauce and it will continue to flavor it. Just before using, scrape all the seeds from inside the bean into the sauce, as these give the flavor and aroma of the bean. This sauce can be kept, well covered, in the refrigerator for up to 4 days.

Poaching Syrup for Pears
or Other Soft Fruits

THIS IS JUST A VARIATION ON SIMPLE SUGAR SYRUP. THE WINE AND LEMON JUICE ADD A BIT OF ACIDITY THAT HELPS TO ACCENTUATE MOST FRUITS' FLAVORS. ONE COULD USE A RED WINE JUST AS WELL, AND IT WOULD COLOR THE FRUIT. **Makes about 9 cups poaching syrup; 8 poached pears** (V)

Bring all the ingredients, except the pears and half of the lemon juice, to a boil in a large pan.

Meanwhile, peel the pears and rub them with the juice of the remaining lemon half to prevent discoloring. Submerge the pears in the poaching liquid and poach at a very gentle rolling boil for 10 to 20 minutes, depending on pear size and ripeness. When the tip of a sharp knife plunges easily through the flesh of the pears, they are done. Remove from the heat and let them cool down in the poaching liquid.

Store the pears in the refrigerator in the liquid, until needed. This syrup can be strained and used again and again.

4 1/2 cups water

4 1/2 cups crisp white wine

4 1/2 cups sugar

1 vanilla bean, split lengthwise

1 clove or several black peppercorns (optional)

juice of 1 lemon

8 ripe pears

Sugar Syrup

THIS BASE SYRUP CAN BE USED FOR SORBETS, POACHING FRUITS, SOAKING SPONGES, AND SO ON.

IT KEEPS INDEFINITELY SO IT IS ONE OF THOSE THINGS TO KEEP ON HAND AS A BASIC IN THE KITCHEN.

Makes about 2 cups Ⓥ

2 cups water

2 cups sugar

1/2 vanilla bean, split lengthwise or 1 teaspoon vanilla extract

2 tablespoons corn syrup (optional)

Place all the ingredients together in a saucepan. Bring to a boil and boil for 2 to 3 minutes. Skim any scum that comes to the surface. This is just impurities being released from the sugar. Remove from the heat and leave to cool. Store in a sealed container in the refrigerator.

Bouquet Garni

THE ADDITION OF A BUNDLE OF HERBS AND OTHER AROMATICS TO SOUPS, BRAISES, AND OTHER DISHES INFUSES THEM WITH A WONDERFUL FRAGRANCE AND SUBTLE FLAVOR AND ALLOWS FOR EASY REMOVAL. Ⓥ

To assemble a simple bouquet garni, gather together 2 or 3 fresh parsley sprigs, a fresh thyme sprig or two, and a bay leaf, and secure with kitchen string. Adjust the composition of the bouquet with other flavorings—celery stalk, leek greens, chervil sprigs—that complement the particular dish you are preparing.

Index